Pruning

GEOFF HODGE

First published in 2008 by
The Crowood Press Ltd
Ramsbury, Marlborough
Wiltshire SN8 2HR

www.crowood.com

British Library Cataloguing-in-Publication Data
A catalogue record for this book is available from the British Library.

ISBN 978 1 86126 986 7

Illustrations by Claire Upsdale

Typeset by Jean Cussons Typesetting, Diss, Norfolk

Printed and bound in Malaysia by Times Offset (M) Sdn Bhd

Contents

CHAPTER 1

To Prune or Not to Prune?

To prune or not to prune, that is the question! To many people just starting out in gardening, the subject of pruning is a difficult one. Which plants need pruning, why do they need pruning, how do you do it, and when? Even experienced gardeners can go cold at the thought of having to prune a plant. Some people think that cutting off the smallest twig is a bit like removing someone's arm and will have the same dire consequences! Luckily, plants are more forgiving than that, and most respond well to pruning and some even thrive on being cut back to ground level. And, of course, there are plants that need little or nothing in the way of regular pruning.

Gardeners can usually be divided into two groups – 'hairdressers' and 'butchers'. The hairdressers are constantly snipping off little bits here and there, titivating their plants to give them a neat overall appearance. The butchers, on the other hand, usually give their plants a good hacking back! In general, it's better to be a butcher than a hairdresser, as constantly tidying up and titivating may make the growth unbalanced, top-heavy or lopsided, and if done at the wrong time, will remove flower buds and result in no display.

So providing you know what you're doing, always a butcher be. But beware, careless and haphazard hacking can easily do more harm than good.

And that's where this book comes in – giving you information on what to do, when and how – the three basics to acquiring green fingers.

WHY PRUNE?

Whenever you pick up the secateurs or pruning saw you must have in your mind a good reason to do so. The main reasons for pruning are:

- To keep a plant to the required size
- To maintain the required shape and habit
- To remove weak, crossing and overcrowded growth
- To remove dead, diseased, dying or damaged growth – the four Ds

Peony bud blast – a disease that is a prime candidate for removal. (Photo: Geoff Hodge)

OPPOSITE: Cutting back dead euphorbia flower heads. (Photo: Tim Sandall)

- To remove reverted growth
- To remove unwanted suckers
- To improve flowering
- To improve fruiting
- To improve foliage and stem growth and/or colour

Remember these reasons before and during any pruning jobs that you tackle – they'll help you decide which parts of the plant need removing. And remember that if a plant is one that needs pruning, it is far better to carry it out regularly when needed rather than leaving it until more major renovation surgery becomes necessary.

In the following chapters on pruning specific plants, no further reference is made to pruning to size, maintaining shape and habit, or removing weak, crossing, overcrowded, reverted, dead,

Conifer dieback. (Photo: Tim Sandall)

diseased, damaged or dying growth or suckers. But these should be the first things you look for, and pay attention to, before attempting to prune for any other reason.

Always start by removing the four Ds; then take weak, crossing, overcrowded and reverted growth; then suckers; and finally, prune to maintain size, shape and habit, and to improve the required attribute (flowers, fruit, foliage and stems).

Pruning to Size

Sadly, cutting to size is often the most usual reason for pruning, because the plant has been put in the wrong place. Where a plant is constantly being cut back because it is growing too tall or wide for the space allotted to it, and as a result, the display is spoilt, it may be better to dig it up and replace it with a plant better suited to the area available.

And be warned: if you did physics at school, you may remember one of the laws of physics – to every action there is an equal and opposite reaction. This often applies to plants, and the pruning law states that the harder and the more often you prune a plant, the stronger it will regrow. So once you start pruning, you may have to get into the habit of doing it regularly.

If a plant has grown too big for its space and is likely to need hard renovation cutting back, bear in mind that such severe pruning may prevent it from performing for a year or two – or seriously weaken it, or even kill it!

However, there are many plants that absolutely thrive on hard pruning, producing vigorous regrowth that flowers in the same year – perfect choices for limited spaces. And there are also numerous dwarf cultivars of many of our popular taller-growing plants that can easily slot into the tightest areas.

Maintaining Shape and Habit

Although many plants look more natural when left to their own devices, there are a lot more that thrive on being pruned to provide a certain effect or shape. And the reverse is also true, in that some plants, especially rampant climbers, look much better if they are strictly trained and pruned accordingly: left to grow unchecked, they soon become a tangled mess.

Even natural-looking plants can produce growth that spoils their look or becomes dangerous, and will need removing. Some trees, for instance, may produce branches that are too low to mow beneath, or could cause an accident if a child, for instance, accidentally ran into them. Some plants need training and pruning from an early age if they are to achieve the desired effect; these include climbers, young trees – especially fruit trees – and hedges. Where initial training is needed it is covered in the entries for the individual plant.

Removing Unwanted Growth

Often pruning can be limited to just removing unwanted growth – weak, crossing and over-crowded stems. Some plants in their natural growth habit produce a mass of weak, thin growth that may become a tangled mess, others do so as a result of being pruned incorrectly. Such growth is unlikely to perform well, and if it is produced in the centre of the plant, can lead to a build-up of pests and disease, as well as being more likely to die back. If allowed to develop, this weak growth can be prone to wind damage, and is also likely to become misshapen as it grows together.

It may be necessary to thin it out to open up the centre of the plant, allowing in more air and light, which in turn will help the stems ripen and conse-quently lead to more flowers and, where appropri-ate, fruit. Where there is excessive growth, two or more branches may cross each other and start rubbing together, causing damage to one or both of them; one or more of the weaker branches should be removed to prevent this. Sometimes branches arising from one side of the plant will grow into its centre and across to the other side; however, this crossing growth is unnecessary as it fills in the middle of the plant and may rub against other branches.

The Four Ds

Growth that is dead is an obvious contender for removal – it serves no use to the plant and is a source of infection for other growth. Anything that is damaged, diseased or starting to die back is similarly ripe for removal; for instance, growth damaged by frost, or by strong or cold winds.

As more people are looking to garden organi-cally, and as fewer chemicals remain available for gardeners to combat pests and disease – especially diseases – pruning out growth that is affected by either of these is often the only way of controlling the problem.

Pests that can be wholly or partially controlled by pruning include aphids (especially woolly aphids), red spider mite, stem-boring caterpillars and scale insects; and diseases include brown rot, canker, coral spot, fire blight, mildew, rust and silver leaf of prunus.

Anything that is affected by the four Ds should be cut far enough back into healthy growth; anything that is irretrievably dead should be completely removed.

Dieback on tree tip. (Photo: Tim Sandall)

Removing Reverted Growth

Plants that are grown for their variegated or other-wise coloured leaves often produce stems whose foliage is all green; this is called reversion. Others that are grown for their curly or twisted stems may produce straight stems. In both cases the offending stem should be pruned out – that is, cut right back to where it originates.

Reverted stems are generally more vigorous, and if left, will soon take over the rest of the plant, spoiling its overall appearance.

Removing Suckers

A sucker is a shoot that arises at or below ground level from a plant's roots or underground stem. Some plants are grafted on to rootstocks in order to control their growth, and in this case a sucker is a shoot that arises from below where the cultivated plant was grafted on to the rootstock (known as the graft union). On standard trees and roses this may be on the main stem.

Many plants are grown as multi-stemmed thickets, where each stem arises from suckers. In these cases the suckers are useful, but stems may need thinning out to prevent overly thick growth. Others, such as sumachs and cherries, produce travelling roots that can produce new shoots a long way from the main plant, and these will need to be removed.

In grafted plants where the sucker arises from the rootstock, such suckers should be removed; they are generally vigorous and may take over the desired cultivar. Rather than remove the sucker by cutting it off, it is usually better to trace it back to where it joins the main root and carefully tear it off. Cutting leaves behind dormant buds that will re-shoot; pulling removes these buds. Plants that are usually grafted include roses, fruit trees, lilac and flowering cherries.

Improving Flowering

Many plants will produce more flowers if they are pruned correctly; pruning encourages the plant to divert its energy into flowering growth and therefore flowers. Some plants will also produce bigger, better flowers if pruned regularly; buddleias are a prime example, producing flower spikes up to three times longer compared to unpruned plants.

Cutting back also ensures the flowers are produced at a height that can be appreciated – as is the case with buddleias and lilacs for instance, which would otherwise tower above your head necessitating stepladders or an upstairs window to appreciate them!

When pruning to improve flowering it is vital to know when the plant flowers, and therefore on what type of growth the buds form and flowers are produced. As a general rule, trees, shrubs and climbers that flower from late autumn and through the winter produce their flowers or flower buds on growth formed that year, and spring and early summer flowerers on growth formed the previous year: these are pruned immediately after flowering. Plants that flower from midsummer into early autumn flower on the current year's growth, and are pruned in early spring, usually just before or just after growth begins.

Naturally there are some exceptions, so always check on the plant in question in the A-Z sections in each chapter.

Improving Fruiting

As flowers produce fruit, it follows that pruning to improve flowering will also improve fruiting. Although you can follow this general principle for ornamental fruit and berries, pruning for edible fruit is a different matter altogether, and usually needs more disciplined pruning. You can find out exactly what needs doing in the chapter on fruit starting on page 115.

Improving Foliage and Stems

Although we usually think about growing plants for their flowers and/or fruit, many are grown for their ornamental, colourful foliage and a few for their attractive stems. Regular pruning of these plants can certainly improve their performance.

Pruning back plants that have become bare in the middle will help produce compact, more vigorous growth with a better covering of leaves. Hard pruning of evergreens rarely affects the size or colour intensity of the foliage, but many deciduous plants grown for their foliage will produce bigger, more colourful leaves if pruned hard annually; good examples include *Catalpa*, *Cotinus*, *Paulownia* and *Sambucus*.

Some *Cornus*, *Rubus* and *Salix* are grown for their colourful winter stems. The colour intensity fades as the stems get older, so annual pruning in spring to remove the oldest stems ensures plenty of fresh, new growth that will colour up well the following winter.

BUYING PLANTS

Probably the most important way of ensuring you get the best out of your plants, and that they grow into healthy specimens that produce the displays you're after, is to buy good plants in the first place. Before parting with your money, take some time to check them over. If you feel brave enough, start by gently knocking them out of their pots to check the roots. You're looking for plenty of healthy, white roots that are not growing round and round the rootball and are potbound – though having said that, it's usually better to buy plants that are slightly potbound as compared to ones that have little or no good root growth.

The top growth should be strong and healthy, with no signs of pest damage, bushy and well balanced and in proportion to the root growth. It is possible to correct growth that is lop-sided or overly long by pruning – but why start with poor plants in the first place?

TOOLS OF THE TRADE

As well as knowing what to do and when, successful pruning also requires a basic tool kit. How much you need depends on the plants you grow, but your kit will generally consist of secateurs, loppers, pruning knife, pruning saw, long-handled/extendable pruners for tall trees, ladders, electric or petrol hedgetrimmer for formal hedges, and maybe even a chainsaw. And the equipment you're using will determine what, if any, safety equipment you need. Thick gloves are almost universal, especially when pruning prickly or thorny plants, but goggles to protect the eyes from wayward stems, and ear defenders when using powered machinery, may also be needed.

Safety

It goes without saying that all pruning equipment can be potentially dangerous, and it pays to treat it with respect. For instance, secateurs should never be carried around in your pockets or tucked into the top of your trousers: rather, use a holster or similar to protect both them and you; and saws should have the blades covered or protected in some way when not in use. Electrical equipment should always be used with an RCD electrical 'trip' device to cut off the power if the cable is cut through.

Also, remember to store all pruning equipment somewhere dry and out of the reach of children.

If you're using a ladder to prune trees, then ensure it is stable and firmly attached to the tree, and preferably have someone else on hand to hold the bottom of it. If you're doing a lot of pruning, a very long hedge or an orchard for instance, it may be worth using scaffolding or a scaffold platform. These are much safer than ladders.

Secateurs

Secateurs are the most important – and most used – pruning tool. There are numerous types and models available, and it pays to pick them up and try them in your hand before buying. A quality pair of secateurs could last you a lifetime, and once you find a pair that suits you, you will want to use them for years.

There is some variation in the stem thickness that secateurs can cope with; always bear this in

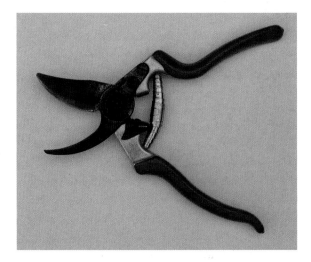

Bypass secateurs. (Photo: Geoff Hodge)

Anvil secateurs. (Photo: Geoff Hodge)

secateurs cut with a scissor action, although only one blade has a cutting edge – although you can get manaresi secateurs for pruning vines that have two cutting blades. Generally speaking, bypass secateurs give the cleanest cuts.

Anvil secateurs have a metal plate or anvil that supports the plant stem while the blade cuts through it. Such secateurs have more of a tendency to crush the stem, but they can give a clean cut.

If you have weak wrists or for some reason find secateurs difficult or tiring to use, try ratchet secateurs. The ratchet causes the secateurs to cut in stages, and very little pressure is needed on the handles.

Remember that secateurs are a precision tool and should only be used for pruning plants – do *not* use them for cutting wire or metal sheet!

Using Secateurs

Secateurs can be used for the following tasks:

mind when pruning, and don't try and force them to cut through anything wider as it's quite easy to damage the plant, the blades and the cutting mechanism.

Apart from size and weight, the only other decision to make is which type, and basically there are only two to choose from – bypass and anvil. Bypass

- Deadheading
- Cutting back annuals, perennials and bulbs
- Cutting flowers for indoor display
- Pruning woody stems up to the recommended diameter

Using loppers. (Photo: Tim Sandall)

When using secateurs, unless cutting very soft material, always position the stem close to the base of the blade, as cutting with the tip can strain the blade(s). Always make a clean, straight cut and without twisting the secateurs or the plant. If the secateurs don't cut through the stem cleanly and easily, then it's probably too big and you should use loppers or a pruning saw.

Loppers

Loppers are simply long-handled secateurs with a wider mouth so they can deal with thicker stems. The handles are around 45cm (18in) long, although telescopic models are available that double the handle length. The longer handles, and the fact that they are used two-handed, provides extra leverage, so more force can be exerted; but the same principles apply as for secateurs, so don't try and cut stems that are too thick.

Make sure the model you buy has shock-absorbing stoppers at the top of the handle because this will prevent jarring and make them far more comfortable to use.

Tree Loppers

Tree loppers, or long-armed pruners, are perfect for getting at high branches where using a ladder or a pair of steps is unsuitable or inadvisable. They comprise a set of bypass secateurs attached to the end of a long pole which may be of a set length, or extendable up to around 3m (10ft). The cutting action is activated either by a lever at the bottom of the pole or via a pulley and cord. You need two hands to use them.

Some models have a rotating head so you can adjust the angle needed to produce a clean cut. Others can have a pruning saw added, so you can cut through thick branches high above your head, and some have a fruit-picking attachment.

Saws

A saw should be used for all thick stems that secateurs or loppers can't cope with. There are numerous types and styles available, and you may decide you need more than one, depending on what you are pruning.

Using long-handled loppers. (Photo: Tim Sandall)

Pruning saws are perfect for cutting through most types of wood, especially living 'green' wood. They have wide-set teeth that make cuts wider than the thickness of the blade, so reducing the risk of jamming. They may have smaller teeth at the tip of the blade to help get you started, with larger teeth nearer the handle to make the major cuts.

A curved pruning saw, or Grecian saw, is usually the best type to have. It has a slightly curved handle and a blade that bites easily into the wood and will cut quickly and cleanly.

A bow saw may be the best choice where very thick branches are involved, especially if these are already dead.

Pruning using a handsaw. (Photo: Tim Sandall)

Shears

Hand shears are the perfect choice for hedges that aren't too large; long hedges are best tackled with a powered hedgetrimmer. But hand shears can also be used on a selection of small-leaved plants where accurate pruning with secateurs isn't necessary; these include box, conifers, lavender and heathers.

As with all pruning tools, you get what you pay for, and it's a good idea to spend money on quality, as you're then guaranteed a pair of shears with blades that will cut well and can be sharpened easily when necessary. Good shears can be heavy,

so test them for weight and balance before you buy. As with loppers, it's important to buy a pair with shock absorbers to prevent jarring of the wrists.

Telescopic-handled shears are available to help reach taller plants. Single-handed shears and sheep-shearing shears are also available, but being one-handed you can't exert as much force, and they are only suitable for very thin growth.

Hedgetrimmers

A powered hedgetrimmer is better than shears where there is a lot of hedge or similar cutting to do, as it is quick and simple to use – though having said that, it is easy to get carried away and remove too much growth, so always pace yourself, and stop and check regularly to see how much growth has been removed.

Hedgetrimmers can be powered by electricity, petrol or even rechargeable batteries, and they come in various blade lengths. Both factors affect how powerful the trimmer is and how quickly it will deal with a hedge, but also how heavy it is; again, check before you buy to make sure you can use it without any difficulty.

Small, electrical shrub pruners are also available for trimming small-leaved plants and for topiary work.

Pruning Knives

Pruning knives aren't used much these days, but they're worth having for cutting back or 'tipping' soft growth, removing rotting and diseased material from branches, and paring the bark smooth after removing larger branches. They're also useful for removing and preparing material for propagating from cuttings.

Chainsaws

Chainsaws are used to cut large branches, and to fell trees and cut them into logs. They are dangerous in the hands of inexperienced and untrained operators: although the machines themselves are now safer than ever, the operator may not be! If you are planning to invest in one, then also invest

Using Bosch shrub shears. (Photo: Geoff Hodge)

in some training and all the correct safety equipment and clothing.

Generally a chainsaw is best left in the hands of a trained expert; if you need to use one, call in a tree surgeon.

CARING FOR YOUR TOOLS

In order for pruning tools to work properly, they need to be cared for. After using secateurs, loppers and shears, use an emery cloth, emery paper or similar to remove caked-on plant material and sap, and then wipe with an oily cloth to prevent rust. Keep all moving parts well lubricated with general household oil.

If you have been pruning plants that are diseased, clean the blades with a suitable disinfectant to avoid spreading the disease from one plant to another.

To ensure the best results and to prevent rough cuts that can help spread disease, all pruning equipment should have sharp blades. Sharpening the blades of secateurs, loppers and shears is quick and easy to do, so invest in an oil or carborundum stone or a handy diamond sharpener.

Saws should be cleaned with care to prevent cutting yourself. They are also more difficult to sharpen; either take them to be sharpened or buy a new blade.

CHAPTER 2

Pruning Techniques

In the first chapter we introduced you to the basics of pruning – the reasons for pruning. But in order to prune correctly it's also important to have an understanding of how plants grow, what pruning does to them, and how they react to pruning. Knowing why you should prune is important, but so is where to prune, how and when. Pruning can be a shock to some plants, especially those that are already under stress or are hacked back to ground level, so it's also important to give them some special care after pruning.

HOW PLANTS GROW

Unlike animals, plants possess very few organs, but those that they do have, serve vital roles, as indicated below.

- Stems, for structure.
- Roots, for stability and to absorb water and minerals from the soil.
- Leaves, to produce food from sunlight (a process known as photosynthesis).
- Flowers, containing the reproductive parts of the plant, and generally used to attract pollinating insects.
- Fruit or seed heads, resulting from successful flower pollination and providing the next generation of plants.
- Buds – the future stems, leaves or flowers in embryonic form.

OPPOSITE: Removing dead fronds from a fern.
(Photo: Geoff Hodge)

Extension growth is usually made just below the uppermost bud on a stem, which is called the apical or terminal bud – the growing point or leader. This bud imposes something called apical dominance: that is, while it is still in place it inhibits the growth of buds below it and on lateral shoots or sideshoots. However, when it is removed, the dominance is lost and buds lower down start to shoot. So cutting back a stem or removing its tip causes buds below to shoot and results in bushier growth.

In some plants, a single sideshoot may grow away strongly and reinstate the apical dominance; in others, two or more growing points share the dominance and produce dual or multiple leaders. In trees this can lead to problems later on, so the weakest leader or leaders should be removed to retain the strongest and/or straightest.

Pulling down a vertical shoot and training it horizontally can also break apical dominance. Sideshoots are produced along the shoot, and these are much more likely to flower and fruit. This technique is particularly useful when training climbers, wall shrubs and several fruit shapes.

PRUNING TECHNIQUES

The following discussion of techniques covers the where and how of pruning. Once you've mastered some basic techniques, you can, with the help of the subsequent chapters, go on to tackle just about any plant in your garden.

Whenever you make a pruning cut it should be done in such a way that the cut heals quickly to prevent disease entering and damaging or killing the plant. Using clean, sharp cutting tools is

Parts of a plant

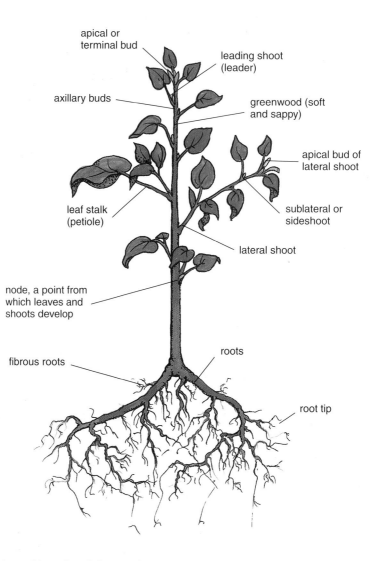

apical or
terminal bud

leading shoot
(leader)

axillary buds

greenwood (soft
and sappy)

apical bud of
lateral shoot

leaf stalk
(petiole)

sublateral or
sideshoot

lateral shoot

node, a point from
which leaves and
shoots develop

roots

fibrous roots

root tip

important here, but so is making the right cut in the right place at the right time.

Timing is essential for ensuring maximum flowering and fruiting (*see* Improving Flowering and Improving Fruiting on page 8) – but other factors may also affect timing. If some evergreens and slightly tender plants are pruned too early in spring, or too late in summer or autumn, the resulting cuts or new growth may be susceptible to frost or cold winds. Moreover there are some plants that will bleed sap, which will weaken them if they are pruned at the wrong time. And some may be more susceptible to disease if pruning is carried out at the wrong time.

When you take your first tentative stems into pruning, you'll probably make a few errors, but don't worry unduly – practice always makes perfect. You'll probably take the 'look once, prune twice' approach, meaning that, unsure what to do, you'll prune a stem and then realize you could have pruned it harder or better. But once you're experienced you'll look twice and then prune only once, like a seasoned professional!

Pruning Cuts

Whenever you take on the pruning challenge, bear in mind that the pruned stem must always end in a

BUD AND SHOOT TYPES

Apical or terminal buds: These appear at the tip of a stem and control its length and growth pattern. If the apical bud is removed or damaged it allows buds lower down to shoot.

Lateral buds: These are usually formed at the nodes — that is, where a leaf joins a stem. They will develop into leaves or sideshoots (laterals), usually in their first year.

Dormant buds: A lateral bud that for one reason or another doesn't come into growth. Pruning a nearby apical bud is likely to stimulate it into growth, producing new leaves or stems.

Adventitious buds (above): These are only produced when damage or pruning occurs and there are no dormant buds nearby. They are only formed when they are needed, producing new leaves or stems, and are often the buds that come into growth when hard renovation pruning is carried out.

In some trees, several buds break at the same point and time, producing a profusion of thin stems called water shoots. In time these will produce useful stems and will flower and fruit normally, but are usually so numerous they crowd one another. In such cases they should either be thinned out or removed completely if not needed.

Vegetative and fruit buds: Vegetative buds are small and thin and go on to produce leaves. Fruit buds are fatter as they contain the embryo flowers. Both can be found on the same stem of plants grown for their edible fruit. By pruning, it is possible to change vegetative buds into fruiting buds, which is why fruit pruning is so important.

Philadelphus before (above) and after (below) pruning. (Photo: Geoff Hodge)

bud, whenever buds are visible. The pruning cut should be clean, with no ragged edges, and should be as near to the bud as possible, but not so close that it damages it.

Growth beyond a bud has nothing to draw the plant's sap beyond that bud, so it will start to wither and will eventually die. The resulting 'snag' may be a source of infection, and may allow disease to travel back through the rest of the stem and kill it.

A bud pointing in a certain direction will produce a shoot that also points in that direction. So, if you prune to an inward-facing bud the resulting shoot will grow inwards and may then cause problems later on if it rubs against other shoots, or causes thick growth that may then encourage disease problems. Outward-facing buds produce shoots that grow out from the plant, but this may result in the plant growing too wide. So always think first, and then choose your bud to prune to.

When pruning plants that produce alternate buds (the first pointing in and the one above pointing out), aim to prune with a slanting cut that slopes away from the bud. This will help shed rainwater, and providing it isn't so oblique that it exposes a large surface area, will help the cut to heal quickly. When pruning plants with opposite buds (a pair of buds opposite each other on different sides of the stem), make a straight cut directly above the pair.

Strange as it may seem, the harder you prune a stem, the more vigorous it regrows. So aim to prune thin, weaker shoots harder than you prune strong stems if you're trying to produce even growth. Strong stems may need only light pruning or tipping back.

Bleeding from Pruning Cuts

Bleeding from pruning cuts, although unsightly and worrying, is not always harmful, although it may delay wound healing. However, in some plants, such as grape vine, it should be avoided as it can severely weaken the plant.

Bleeding occurs due to the pressure of the sap within the water-conductive tissues of the stem. There are no practical measures to stop the bleeding, although putting melted candle or sealing wax over the wound may help in some cases.

Plants prone to bleeding include *Acer, Betula, Carpinus, Juglans, Laburnum, Magnolia, Morus, Populus, Sophora, Tilia* and *Vitis.*

The timing and individual requirements of each plant should always be checked in the relevant A–Z sections to prevent severe bleeding.

DEADHEADING

Plants produce flowers for just one reason – to produce seeds and so propagate themselves. Once seed has been set, the plant stops flowering as its job is done.

However, unless you want to keep the seeds for sowing or to enjoy the resulting fruit or seedheads, it is a good idea to deadhead – to remove the faded flower and the developing seedhead or capsule below it. This is because the plant channels energy into the development of the seeds, slowing further growth and reducing flower development. Regular deadheading directs that energy into stronger growth and improved flowering performance.

Obviously on large shrubs and trees this isn't practical, but on other plants, especially annuals, bedding plants, bulbs and roses, particularly those in containers, hanging baskets and prominent positions in the garden, you'll dramatically extend the floral display if you do.

On many plants you will be able to use thumb and forefinger to snap off the faded flower where it joins the stem. With most woody plants, however, you will probably have to use secateurs; make sure you cut just above a bud or growth point, and make sure you don't damage buds or developing growth immediately below the flower.

Pinch pruning. (Photo: Geoff Hodge)

PINCH PRUNING

Pinch pruning, sometimes called finger and thumb pruning, involves removing soft shoot tips and is a useful technique for producing bushy growth or removing unwanted young or soft growth. As shoots age and possibly become harder, the finger and thumb may have to be replaced with a sharp pruning knife or even secateurs.

Although it can be used on a wide range of woody plants when growth is young and soft, it is particularly used on bedding plants and half-hardy perennials, such as argyranthemums, chrysanthemums, coleus (*Solenostemon*), fuchsias and pelargoniums.

It is a particularly useful technique for removing flowering shoots from plants that are mainly grown for their foliage; once they come into flower the quality of the foliage may be reduced. Constantly pinching back flowering plants will delay their flowering, but once pinching stops, and because lots of sideshoots have been produced as a result, the flowering display can be spectacular.

DISBUDDING

Many flowering and fruiting plants, if left to their own devices, produce a profusion of small flowers and fruit. But you can remove some, or nearly all of the flower buds when they're still small to allow the plant to produce fewer but larger specimens. This is common on carnations, chrysanthemums, dahlias and roses, especially for exhibition purposes where biggest is best!

ROOT PRUNING

Pruning plant roots is a drastic solution, but often a necessary one; it can restrain excessive growth, or bring young trees and shrubs into flower and fruit when less severe measures are ineffective. Pruning roots reduces vigour and so promotes the formation of flowers instead of leafy growth. Very mature plants should not be root pruned, except as a last resort, as they have less resilience than young ones.

Root pruning of trees and of old, large shrubs is probably best carried out over two years, in winter, removing half the roots at a time. It's a simple matter of digging a trench around the tree, 30–40cm (12–16in) deep and wide, and about 1.2m (4ft) from the trunk. Refill the trench, stake the tree if appropriate, and make sure it is well watered in subsequent summers.

A milder effect, and more suited to shrubs and even to climbers, can be achieved by inserting a spade to its full depth around the plant to cut the surface roots. Make the cut in a circle at the spread of the plant's branches. If this doesn't work, root pruning can be repeated the following year working more closely to the plant – 50cm (20in) from the stem. This type of root pruning is best carried out when the plant is dormant, from late autumn until late winter.

Plants growing in pots are easily root pruned. In this case up to 20 per cent of the roots can be shortened by about a quarter, and the other roots trimmed to ensure the plant will fit back into the pot. Then replant it in fresh compost, preferably with added controlled-release fertilizer, and water well.

SPECIALIZED PRUNING TECHNIQUES

As well as general pruning, there are a couple of more specialized pruning techniques you can use – coppicing or stooling, and pollarding.

Coppicing (Stooling)

Coppicing, also known as stooling, is the technique of cutting back shrubs and trees to ground level or just above to encourage new shoots. It is particularly useful to promote colourful juvenile stems, ornamental foliage, and to rejuvenate plants that tolerate hard pruning.

Dogwoods and some willows, such as *Salix alba* var. *vitellina* 'Britzensis', are grown for their colourful stems. The best colour comes from one- or two-year-old wood. To ensure a continuous supply, it is necessary to shorten all the stems to within 5–7.5cm (2–3in) of the ground, or to the previous year's stubs in spring each year.

Some *Cornus*, such as 'Midwinter Fire', can be weak growers on poor soils, so cut out just one-third of the stems each year; the remaining stems will probably not be as richly coloured, but they will be stronger.

Coppicing to a stump about 60cm (2ft) tall in early spring can have a dramatic effect on some plants. It restricts the size of trees such as *Paulownia* and *Catalpa*, producing a cluster of stems, and causes the leaves to grow larger than usual. A similar treatment of *Eucalyptus gunnii* encourages round juvenile foliage that is more striking than the elongated adult leaves.

Overgrown yews, hazels and hornbeams can be cut close to the ground in late winter. This results in the production of lots of new stems that can be thinned to make an airy bush once more. Hazels, in particular, are coppiced every few years to produce straight canes, and these can be used as plant supports in the garden.

Pollarding

Pollarding is similar, but here the head of the main branches is cut back to promote more bushy foliage growth and to prevent the tree outgrowing its allotted space. Pollarding, or reclaiming a lapsed pollard, can be a tricky job and it may be better to have the work done by a tree surgeon.

Pollards can be recognized by the fact that they have numerous branches originating at the same point on the tree. These shoots emerge from dormant buds under the bark, or adventitiously from wounds. Initially the new branches are held weakly in place because they grow from under the bark rather than from within the tree. Over a number of years a noticeably swollen 'pollard head' forms where new shoots spring up each year. Shoots growing from the pollard are removed while the wood is young, close to the base of the new growth.

Trees that respond well to this treatment include some species of *Acer*, *Alnus*, *Fraxinus*, *Liriodendron*, *Morus*, *Platanus*, *Quercus*, *Tilia* and *Ulmus*.

The best time for pollarding is in late winter or early spring. Pollarding is best started on young trees, as young wood responds rapidly to wounding, reducing the risk of decay. Initially the tree is grown to the desired height and branch framework.

Once pollarded, it is important to continue the cycle of cutting. The weight and angle of the new branches can lead to weakness, particularly where many branches are crowded together.

Branches should be cut above the previous pollarding cuts in order to avoid exposing older wood, which may be at increased risk of decay. In some cases it is preferable to leave some living branches intact, or to cut above a side branch.

POST-PRUNING DEPRESSION

Pruning, especially hard pruning, can be quite a shock to plants, especially if they have been allowed to get on with it and have never been pruned before, or if they're under stress. That's why some special care after pruning is always necessary.

Plants store excess food in their stems and branches, so cutting these away reduces their food supplies. After pruning, it's always a good idea to give the plants a good feed with a fertilizer. Liquid feeds will give a quick boost, but are short-lived; granular feeds last much longer, and controlled-release fertilizers will feed the plants for several months. Most flowering trees, shrubs and climbers respond well to feeding with a granular rose fertilizer. A plant's feeder roots are roughly distributed at the edge of the branch canopy, and the feed should be spread in a circle in this area – not thrown at the base of the stems where it will be wasted, as this area contains few feeding roots.

After feeding, water the soil and give the area around the plant a thick mulch of organic matter, such as well-rotted manure, garden compost, composted bark, mushroom compost or whatever you usually use.

Treating Pruning Cuts

Many gardeners panic about leaving pruning cuts uncovered, especially large ones; quite rightly they believe they are points where disease can enter and cause damage. However, providing the cut has been made cleanly and correctly, the wound should heal itself, and there is no need to use a wound sealant. Such healants don't assist the plant's healing process and can, in some cases, even hinder it. Large cuts with rough, jagged edges should be made smooth with a pruning knife, but without enlarging the wound.

For more information on making large pruning cuts on trees, *see* Removing Large Branches on page 89.

DEALING WITH PRUNINGS

After pruning, it's likely that you will have a large pile of stems to deal with. Rather than waste these by disposing of them or even burning them, the best course of action is to cut them into small pieces with secateurs, or to shred them in a shredder, and add them to the compost heap. The smaller the pieces and the larger their surface area, the quicker they will rot down. To aid decomposition, it's a good idea to add a high-nitrogen granular fertilizer or even grass clippings to the cuttings.

If you don't have a compost heap, it is possible to add the shreddings direct to border soil, but because this can reduce nutrients in the soil, always add a fertilizer to replace them. Conifer and other resinous shreddings are best composted, as they can 'poison' the soil and the plants growing in it.

KEEP WITHIN THE LAW

Trees, conifer hedges and large wayward plants can cause problems with neighbours, and if the situation is not handled carefully and correctly it can lead to legal disputes.

You are within your rights to cut back any plant that is growing over a recognized boundary. Any part of a plant – both above and below ground – can be cut back to the boundary, provided it does not cause undue damage to the plant, and provided you ask the owner of the plant if they want to have the prunings returned, as technically these still belong to them!

High hedges that restrict access to light are often the subject of legal battles; find out more about 'High Hedges' on page 113.

Some trees, especially those in areas of outstanding natural beauty, may be covered by Tree Preservation Orders (TPOs); such trees are covered by law, and it is illegal to carry out any pruning without permission from the council or issuing body. For more information, *see* page 90.

CHAPTER 3

Annuals, Herbaceous Perennials and Bulbs

For some reason, the pruning of annuals and perennials is left out of most pruning books – but not this one. Because of the soft, non-woody growth they produce and the way they grow, 'pruning' isn't a major part of their maintenance. But they nearly all respond well to some type of pinching or cutting back, and especially to regular deadheading.

DEADHEADING

As pointed out on page 18, deadheading can help keep plants flowering for a prolonged time, as well as looking attractive for longer. This is especially true with annuals and herbaceous perennials, including the half-hardy perennial bedding plants that make up so much of our summer displays.

Most summer annuals and half-hardy perennials can flower continuously from early summer right through until the first hard frosts in autumn with regular deadheading – or only for a few weeks without. The choice is yours! Even winter- and spring-flowering bedding plants, such as pansies, primroses and polyanthus, produce longer displays when the faded flowers are removed.

As these plants use a lot of energy to provide colourful displays for months on end, access to plenty of nutrients is also essential. This can be done by feeding with a suitable liquid fertilizer every ten to fourteen days, or by adding a controlled-release fertilizer when planting out.

Because their stems are soft, most deadheading can be done with thumb and forefinger. Others

OPPOSITE: Antirrhinum in flower. (Photo: Geoff Hodge)

Dianthus before (above) and after (below) deadheading. (Photo: Geoff Hodge)

need to be cut with a knife (with care), scissors or secateurs. As always, remember to try and 'prune' to a bud, sideshoot or growth point. For plants such as pelargoniums that produce their flowers on top of long stems, this means tracing the flowering stem down to where it joins the main stem and carefully removing it there; pelargonium stems usually come off cleanly and easily by bending them away from the main stem.

Some perennials may not flower again that year after deadheading; others, especially those that start flowering early in the year, including *Astrantia*, delphiniums, hardy geraniums, lupins, *Phlox* and pinks (*Dianthus*), will reward you with further flushes of flowers later on.

Of course some perennials, such as grasses, Chinese lantern (*Physalis*), cornflower (*Centaurea*), globe thistle (*Echinops*), golden rod (*Solidago*), honesty (*Lunaria*), *Iris foetidissima*, Michaelmas daisy (*Aster*), sunflower (*Helianthus*) and yarrow (*Achillea*) produce ornamental seed heads, and all or some of these can be kept in place to enhance the garden in autumn and winter. Many will provide important food sources for birds.

Fuchsia 'Diana, Princess of Wales'. *(Photo: Geoff Hodge)*

HALF-HARDY PERENNIALS

There is a wide range of half-hardy perennials that are planted out in late spring or early summer to provide masses of summer colour to beds, borders and containers. The following are all popular types that respond well to deadheading:

Angelonia
Argyranthemum (marguerites)
Felicia amelloides (blue daisy)
Fuchsia (upright and trailing fuchsias)
Gazania
Heliotropium (heliotrope, cherry pie)
Osteospermum (African daisy)
Pelargonium (bedding geraniums and trailing geraniums)
Petunia (trailing Surfinia and other types)
Scaevola (fan flower)

ANNUALS

As well as deadheading, annuals may need pinching back to help induce bushier growth. This can sometimes be carried out when they are young seedlings, especially if they are growing tall and lanky, or later in the growing period. Pinching back will delay flowering, but ensures stronger plants with more flowering sideshoots and so a much better, flower-packed display.

PERENNIALS INCLUDING FERNS

Herbaceous perennials produce rootstocks, rhizomes or tuberous roots from which new foliage and their flowering stems are produced annually. Winter- and spring-flowering species should have their flower heads, or flowering stems and any dead, dying or diseased growth, removed after flowering. Replacement growth that will flower the following year can usually be seen at this time and should be left alone.

Most perennials flower in summer or autumn. Their pruning is carried out in late autumn when flowering has finished, and the stems and foliage are turning yellow or brown. This involves cutting down all the dead and dying growth to ground level. Those that produce attractive seed heads can be left until late winter or early spring.

Perennials that produce leaves and flower stems from below soil level, such as peonies, are cut back to soil level. Perennials that produce new basal shoot growth, such as asters and *Sedum spectabile*, are cut back less severely; sedums should be pruned carefully so as not to damage their new growth. Evergreen herbaceous plants will only need to have the old flower spikes and individual damaged growth removed. Plants that produce very soft growth, such as hostas, die back completely; no pruning is needed, just carefully remove the leaves once fully dead.

Cutting back can be left until early spring; in a severe winter the dead foliage and stems give protection to the young basal shoots. However, more care is needed when cutting back at this time to avoid damaging new shoot growth. Although most shrubs are fed after cutting back, all perennials should be fed in spring.

Brunnera macrophylla 'Jack Frost'. *(Photo: Geoff Hodge)*

Cutting back a fern. (Photo: Geoff Hodge)

Fresh foliage

Some herbaceous plants that look great in spring often start to decline by summer. Their foliage starts to look very tatty, often diseased or ravaged by slugs and other pests; good examples of this include *Brunnera*, *Lamium* and *Pulmonaria*. Similarly, some early summer-flowering plants look the same, especially catmint (*Nepeta*), lady's mantle (*Alchemilla*) and oriental poppies (*Papaver orientale*). To bring them back to their former glory, simply shear off all the old foliage, feed with a granular fertilizer and water well. Within a few weeks they will be covered with fresh new foliage.

The Chelsea Chop

The Chelsea chop is an innovative method of cutting back perennials to promote later flowering; it also makes staking unnecessary on taller species as it reduces their overall size. In effect it is lengthening the flowering period by a type of deadheading – but before the plant starts to flower!

To produce this look, some flowering stems are cut back by a quarter, some by a half, and others by up to three-quarters, resulting in layers of flowers. It is called the Chelsea chop because often the best time to do it is during or just after the RHS Chelsea Flower Show at the end of May.

It can be used on a number of mid- to late-flowering perennials such as *Anthemis*, *Aster novi-belgii*, some campanulas, *Coreopsis*, *Echinacea*, *Helenium*, *Helianthus*, *Macleaya*, *Monarda*, *Phlox*, *Rudbeckia* and *Sedum*. This is a new technique that is definitely worth experimenting with.

ORNAMENTAL GRASSES, SEDGES AND RUSHES

Deciduous grasses, which die back to their roots in

autumn or winter, should be cut back hard each year, preferably in autumn once the flowering stems have died. Some gardeners like to leave the faded flower stems in place to provide autumn and winter interest, and food for birds. In some slightly tender grasses, leaving the dead growth in place over winter may provide some degree of frost protection for the roots. However, leaving the dead growth in place can provide homes for pests and diseases, in which case cutting back in late winter is an option.

Cutting back in spring can be tricky if it is left too late, as there is always the possibility of cutting through the new, emerging growth.

Whenever cutting back is carried out, the aim for most grasses should be to cut to within 5–10cm (2–4in) of the ground, depending on the growth produced. The easiest way is to use a pair of shears. Start by cutting back to around 25–30cm (10–12in), and clear away the trimmings and other dead material. You will now have a better view of the centre of the plant and can cut back harder as necessary and to make a more rounded plant. Finish by carefully pulling out any low-growing dead material.

Evergreen grasses may not need any tidying up, apart from carefully teasing out dead growth. Any trimming that is needed is best done in spring.

Pruning a banana plant. (Photo: Geoff Hodge)

BANANAS

Even so called hardy bananas, like *Musa basjoo*, can be badly affected by winter cold and wet if left outside all year. As a result, in spring they often have lots of dead or dying leaves and leaf bases that need careful removing with secateurs and/or a pruning knife.

In hot summers they may flower, but they rarely produce fruit. After flowering the stem will die, but will have been replaced by new shoots from ground level, and this should be cut down to the ground to allow the new stems to develop.

TREE FERNS

Unless the top of the fern is being protected with straw or similar material in winter, there is no need to remove any fronds during winter, unless they are frost damaged or are dying back naturally. During the growing season damaged fronds can be removed as new fronds are continuously produced.

BULBS AND BULBOUS PLANTS

The only pruning that most bulbs need is dead-heading after flowering – and make sure you remove the developing seed pod as well as the withered flower. After flowering the foliage of many bulbs can start to deteriorate, look untidy or simply get in the way of other plants. The temptation is always to cut down the foliage or, especially with daffodils, to tie it in neat knots. However, avoid the temptation at all costs, and keep the foliage in place until it starts to die down naturally.

With bulbous plants such as cannas, dahlias and lilies that produce quite strong stems, you will need to cut these down to ground level (or 15cm (6in) above it for dahlias) in the autumn. For all the others, carefully pulling the dead foliage away should suffice, and if the foliage doesn't come away cleanly with a gentle tug, leave it alone until it does.

Most bulbs need to build up their strength after flowering to ensure they are strong enough to flower the following year, and they need their foliage to do this. The leaves are the plant's power-house, and if you remove them the bulb will be weak and unlikely to flower, or will flower poorly the following year. Rather than remove the foliage you should therefore do everything to keep it healthy and growing for as long as possible. Watering and feeding during and just after flowering will give the best results. Liquid feeds are better, and those that also act as a foliar feed are better still.

Providing you have kept the plants well fed and watered, and if you really must remove the foliage before it dies down naturally, you should wait for at least eight weeks after flowering before cutting it off.

Cutting back dead tulip growth. (Photo: Geoff Hodge)

CHAPTER 4

Shrubs

Shrubs are the backbone of the garden. They provide the majority of its structure, as well as year-long or seasonal displays from foliage, flowers, fruit and even stem colour.

Most shrubs are long-lived and provide many years of enjoyment. But to ensure they maintain their health and produce displays for as long as possible, many will need to be pruned, often annually. But equally, there are just as many shrubs that need little or nothing in the way of regular pruning, apart from cutting to size and shape and removing unwanted growth.

The aim is always to remove the oldest, less productive growth, provide room for younger growth that will perform better, and help produce and promote healthy new growth to ensure the plant's longevity.

Initial pruning, and even some training just after planting or in the first year, is often necessary to prevent plants becoming tall and straggly; whenever this is needed, it is given in the A–Z section (see page 30).

As young plants grow they may be lightly pruned to help improve their shape. Tip pruning by pinching out the soft growth tips, or cutting back long leading shoots or sideshoots by up to one-third, will help encourage branching lower down and will result in a bushier plant. Of course, if a single dominant shoot is needed, maybe to produce a small, single-leader tree or a standard, then any cutting back of the main stem should be delayed until the plant reaches the desired height.

OPPOSITE: *Callistemon viminalis* 'Captain Cook'.
(*Photo: Tim Sandall*)

MAINTENANCE PRUNING

To get the most out of your shrubs, remember the principles of 'Why prune?', as detailed in Chapter 1 (see page 5). As always, this should be your first reason for getting out the secateurs. Then prune, if necessary, following the information in the A–Z section that follows.

Also remember the pruning techniques described in Chapter 2 on page 15, making the correct types of cut, deadheading where necessary or possible, using any specialized pruning techniques, and finally curing the post-pruning depression.

SHRUBS AS STANDARDS

If the training and pruning bug hits you hard, you may want to try your hand at training shrubs as standards – that is, on a clear single stem with a bushy head. Such plants give height to a border and raise the plant's decorative features to eye level where they can be better enjoyed.

Standards will need staking during their formative years; a bamboo cane is usually sufficient in the early years, but a wooden stake may be needed as the plant gets older, depending on the size and weight of the head. Some standards will need permanent staking.

Select plants with a single strong shoot or leader, or prune away any other shoots to provide a single leader. Keep the leader growing well, removing sideshoots as they form, but keeping all leaves that grow on the leader until it is slightly taller than the desired height. Then pinch out the growing point; this will induce the next few buds below to break and start forming the branches of the head.

Allow the sideshoots in the head to grow for one year, and then reduce them by half. Once sideshoots start to form on these shoots they, too, can be cut back to start forming a bushy head.

Further pruning should be done at the right time, following the information for each plant in the A–Z section, to keep the head bushy and flowering or fruiting as expected. Sideshoots on the main stem should be removed or, better still, rubbed out as buds, as soon as possible.

SHRUBS A–Z

Abelia × grandiflora 'Francis Mason'.
(Photo: Tim Sandall)

Abelia
Evergreen/deciduous
This colourful shrub produces its flowers in summer on the previous year's growth, and may also flower again later on the current year's growth.

In spring, after the last frosts, remove any dead, diseased or damaged growth and any spindly shoots. After flowering, remove up to one in four of the oldest flowered shoots, cutting back to strong new shoots or even to just above ground level.

To renovate old plants, cut stems down to their base in early spring.

Acer japonicum, A. palmatum
Japanese maple
Deciduous
Japanese maples are grown for their highly ornamental foliage, which often produces colourful autumn shades.

They don't need much in the way of pruning, and in fact prefer not to be pruned regularly. Any pruning should be carried out in winter when the plant is fully dormant, otherwise it can bleed. Small cuts to remove reverted shoots can also be made in late summer/early autumn.

When the plants are young, a little light pruning may help to produce lower branches and hence a bushier shape. Badly placed or crossing stems can be removed in winter. Plants may produce some dieback in winter, which should also be removed to prevent the plant looking unsightly.

For pruning tree maples, *see* page 91.

Amelanchier
Snowy mespilus
Deciduous
Amelanchiers are grown for their attractive young foliage, white flowers in spring, and attractive autumnal leaf colour and fruit. They can be grown as multi-stemmed bushes or trained as small trees.

When growing as a multi-stemmed shrub, all that is needed is to thin out one in three of the oldest stems in winter to prevent the plant becoming congested in the middle. This is how you renovate neglected plants, too.

To grow as a tree, select the straightest, strongest stem and remove all sideshoots to create a trunk from 60cm–1.8m (2–6ft). Then allow a branched head to form, selecting and retaining sideshoots to create an evenly spaced framework; all others can be removed.

Aralia
Devil's walking stick
Deciduous
Aralias are large, suckering shrubs with handsome foliage and large panicles of flowers.

Once established, keep pruning to a minimum apart from removing damaged, dead or misplaced growth in spring. Late frosts may damage the growing tip, in which case cut back to a healthy sideshoot. Variegated cultivars may produce reverted shoots, which should be removed.

Arbutus
Strawberry tree
Evergreen
Arbutus is grown for its handsome dark green foliage, flowers, strawberry-like fruit and rusty-coloured peeling bark.

Plants may be prone to frost damage, so prune this out once new growth can be seen. The pruning of established plants is best kept to a minimum, although weak growth and branches that die off within the leaf canopy should be removed.

A. andrachne, A × andrachnoides and *A. menziesii* are often grown as trees. In this instance keep the central leading shoot and remove low sideshoots if necessary to display the main trunk.

Old, neglected plants usually respond to hard pruning in spring.

Artemisia
Wormwood
Evergreen/deciduous
Artemisias are grown for their attractive, aromatic, silvery foliage.

Regular pruning is needed to prevent them becoming bare and leggy at the base and to produce bushy growth. Prune in early to mid-spring, after the danger of frost has passed.

Cut back all stems to 5cm (2in) from the ground in the first spring after planting. Thereafter, cut back the previous year's growth by up to half each year, and remove any growth damaged by winter weather. You can help keep the plants bushy by regularly pinching out the shoot tips of new growth throughout the summer.

To renovate overgrown plants, cut back all stems hard in mid-spring.

Aucuba
Spotted laurel
Evergreen
Aucubas are mainly grown for their leathery, glossy foliage, which in some cultivars is highly variegated. They also produce white flowers in summer and red berries on female cultivars.

Aucubas naturally produce dense growth, but they can become straggly, dying back after cold winters and becoming bare at the base.

In the first spring after planting, it's a useful tip to cut back the previous year's growth by around one-third to encourage bushiness. Once established, remove any overlong, wayward and straggly shoots and winter dieback in mid-spring, after the winter display of berries on fruiting forms. These can be cut back to strong buds or sideshoots or to the main stem. Reverted stems on variegated cultivars should be removed completely.

Plants that have become old and neglected, or bare at the base, can be rejuvenated by cutting back stems to their base. Do this over three years, removing one in three stems each year.

For pruning hedges, *see* page 109.

Berberis
Evergreen and deciduous
Berberis bear lots of yellow or orange flowers in spring on the previous year's growth, followed by red or black fruit in autumn. Many of the deciduous types also produce excellent autumn leaf colour. Regular pruning isn't necessary.

The evergreen types can be pruned after flowering, if the berries are not wanted; otherwise prune in late autumn or winter after the berries have gone. As evergreens become older, flowering and fruiting is restricted to the edges of the plant, in which case hard pruning may be needed; cut back all stems to within 30cm (12in) of their base in late winter, although the following year's flowers will be lost.

Aucuba Japonica 'Crotonifolia'. *(Photo: Tim Sandall)*

The deciduous forms are best thinned out each year after flowering to a low framework of permanent branches, removing some shoots down to their base. This encourages better leaf colour, important in purple-leaved cultivars, and attractively coloured young stems. Those grown for autumn colour shouldn't be pruned like this as the best leaf colour is produced on older stems. Deciduous plants can be renovated in the same way as the evergreen ones.

For pruning hedges, *see* page 109.

Brachyglottis (Dunedin Group) 'Sunshine' (*Senecio* 'Sunshine')

Evergreen

This attractive shrub is grown for its silvery-grey foliage and yellow summer flowers produced on the previous year's growth.

Prune in spring as new growth starts to break and the worst of the winter frosts are over. Check for winter damage and remove any affected growth, plus any wayward and thin branches. Hard pruning at this time to encourage a compact bushy shape will result in a better foliage effect, but at the expense of flowers. Plants can also be pruned to shape after flowering.

Neglected, overgrown plants can be cut back hard in spring, cutting back to buds on old wood. Very old plants rarely reshoot successfully and are best replaced.

Buddleja davidii

Butterfly bush
Deciduous

Buddleias are grown for their attractive, highly scented flowers, which are excellent for attracting wildlife. These are produced on the current year's growth in summer. One or two cultivars have variegated foliage. Plants can become leggy and flowerless if left unpruned.

The main pruning should be carried out in spring, when new growth can be seen, and after the danger of hard frosts.

In the first spring after planting, prune out any weak growth and shorten main stems to produce a low framework of branches 15–60cm (6–24in) high, depending on how tall you want the plant to be. Thereafter, prune back to this framework annually, cutting back the previous year's growth to two or three buds. Shorten new growth from the base by up to three-quarters, or remove it completely if the overall growth is too dense.

As plants mature, it pays to cut out any dead or unproductive parts of the framework.

Deadhead as the flowers fade, cutting back to a pair of strong shoots. In windy areas, it also pays to shorten the top growth by about one-third in autumn to prevent root rock.

Old, neglected plants usually respond well to cutting back hard in spring as new growth is breaking.

Buddleja alternifolia. (Photo: Geoff Hodge)

Other *Buddleja* species

Buddleja alternifolia carries clusters of scented, lilac flowers in early summer on the previous year's stems. This should be pruned in summer, immediately after flowering, cutting back the flowered stems to healthy buds or non-flowered sideshoots.

Neglected plants can also be cut back hard.

Buddleja globosa (orange ball tree) produces round orange flowers on the previous year's growth. It doesn't need regular pruning, but when required this should be done in later winter before new growth appears. Only prune out one-third of the length of wayward and very tall branches, otherwise all the coming year's display will be lost – although these will flower well the following year.

Buxus
Box
Evergreen

This is a tough evergreen often used for formal hedging and topiary. It responds well to clipping and readily shoots from old wood.

Cut back young plants quite hard to encourage bushy growth. Trim mature plants any time from early to late summer; two cuts per summer will encourage strong, bushy growth.

Old, neglected plants usually respond well to hard pruning in late spring, and can even be cut back to within 15–30cm (6–12in) of the ground.

For pruning hedges, *see* page 109.

Callicarpa
Beauty berry
Deciduous

The beauty berry is grown for its unusual violet fruit produced on new as well as older wood.

It doesn't need regular pruning, but thinning out older stems to their base will prevent the plant becoming congested and so help display the berries to better effect. Remove one in three or one in four of the older stems in spring after the risk of severe frost, but before growth starts.

Callicarpas will normally respond to hard pruning, cutting all stems back to their base. Those that look as if they have been killed by cold weather should recover if the dead growth is cut back to ground level in spring.

Callistemon
Bottlebrush
Evergreen

Callistemons produce lax, arching stems; the bottlebrush flowers are borne on the ends of new growth in summer.

After planting, tip-prune new plants to encourage bushy growth. Mature plants are best left unpruned, but in time can become straggly. To help prevent this, cut back older stems to young shoots after flowering.

Although callistemons will respond well to hard pruning, this should be limited and spread over several years, and no more than one in three stems should be cut back each year.

Calluna
Ling
Evergreen

These low-growing ground-cover shrubs are covered in colourful flowers any time from summer to autumn.

They should be pruned annually after flowering to keep them compact and to ensure long life and long flowering. Simply shear off all the old flower-

Camellia × *williamsii* 'Donation'. *(Photo: Tim Sandall)*

ing stems, together with some of the leafy growth below. Never cut back into old wood as plants rarely recover. Straggly plants past their best should be replaced.

Very dwarf varieties are best not pruned at all, but cut out overlong shoots to their point of origin.

Camellia
Evergreen
Grown for their large, blowsy flowers that are mainly produced in late winter or spring, and for their glossy foliage, camellias can also be grown as wall shrubs. Being early flowering, they flower on the previous year's growth.

Young plants can be pruned to produce bushy growth by cutting back thin or leggy shoots to two or three buds – or by removing them completely.

Established plants don't require regular pruning, but can be kept bushy by pruning immediately after flowering, and preferably before the growth buds break.

Old and overgrown plants can be renovated by hard pruning in early spring; cut back stems to around 60cm (2ft) from ground level, or even harder if they are healthy and there are signs of growth. Such severe pruning is best carried out over three years, cutting back one in three of the main branches each year.

Camellia sasanqua is an autumn-flowering species, but is treated in the same way.

Caragana
Deciduous
This shrub is grown for its attractive, pea-like flowers produced on short shoots on two-year-old wood.

Prune young plants to encourage bushy growth. No further pruning is needed.

Carpenteria
Evergreen
This is a spectacular plant producing large white flowers in summer on the previous year's growth. Sadly it can tend to become leggy.

Prune after flowering to maintain bushiness, and remove one in three of the older stems that have

Caryopteris × clandonensis before (left) and after (right) pruning. (Photo: Geoff Hodge)

been weakened by flowering, cutting them out at the base.

More drastic pruning is often possible, but not recommended as plants take a long time to recover.

Caryopteris
Blue spiraea
Deciduous
Caryopteris is grown mainly for its blue flowers produced in summer and autumn on the current year's growth, but also for its ornamental grey-green foliage. In cold winters most, or all of the previous year's growth can die back.

In the first spring after planting, prune plants hard to produce a low framework, preferably on a short leg. *Caryopteris* is best pruned annually in mid- to late spring as the growth buds are breaking; when dead wood is more obvious, prune to the resulting framework of branches. This prevents the plant becoming bare at the base as well as promoting flowering shoots. Shorten all stems to within 2.5–5cm (1–2in) of the older wood. Do not cut into the older wood, as plants rarely reshoot from old growth.

To renovate neglected plants, cut them back in late spring to the lowest active growth you can see – but be prepared for them to fail.

Ceratostigma
Hardy plumbago
Deciduous and evergreen
Despite its name, *Ceratostigma* isn't completely hardy and often dies back to ground level. It produces its powdery-blue flowers from midsummer to autumn on the current year's growth. The foliage produces colourful red tints in autumn.

All pruning should be carried out in mid-spring. If plants die back in winter, remove all dead wood and cut back remaining stems to within 2.5–5cm (1–2in) from ground level. If plants retain a woody framework after winter, treat as for *Caryopteris.*

Chaenomeles
Flowering or Japanese quince, japonica
Deciduous
This hardy shrub produces a colourful floral display in spring, on growth produced the previous year, followed by large quince-like fruit in autumn.

Once established, *Chaenomeles* needs little in the way of regular pruning, apart from removing shoots that crowd out the centre of the plant. If the plant isn't flowering well, shortening new growth in summer to five to seven leaves will improve performance. Pruning should be done in late spring or early summer after flowering.

Plants can be renovated by hard pruning, although this is best carried out over two to three years.

For pruning as a wall shrub, *see* page 67; for pruning hedges, *see* page 109.

Chimonanthus
Wintersweet
Deciduous or semi-evergreen
A beautifully scented, winter-flowering shrub that only flowers when plants are five to seven years old on the previous year's growth.

Wintersweet is best left unpruned, especially when young so that it can build up plenty of mature flowering growth. Even when established, little or no pruning is needed. If necessary, shoots can be thinned and older growth can be shortened by up to 30cm (12in) after flowering, but keep this to a minimum or the following winter's display will be reduced.

Hard pruning can delay flowering by several years and is best avoided.

Choisya
Mexican orange blossom
Evergreen
This evergreen produces attractive, glossy foliage and highly scented flowers in spring, although it may flower sporadically throughout the year.

Little or no regular pruning is needed, although cutting back those shoots that have flowered in spring can help encourage further flowering in autumn and winter. Frosted shoots can also be dealt with at the same time.

Choisyas can become top-heavy in time, and hard pruning in spring can help produce tidier, bushier plants.

Cistus
Sun rose, rock rose
Evergreen
Colourful small shrubs, often used for medium-sized ground cover, covered in individually short-lived flowers in summer.

After planting, plants can be pruned to encourage bushiness; certainly any tall shoots are best cut back by up to two-thirds to sideshoots.

Established plants need little or no pruning, but dead and damaged shoots can be removed after flowering, together with any wayward growth.

Old, neglected plants don't respond well to being cut back hard.

Clerodendrum trichotomum 'Carnival'.
(Photo: Geoff Hodge)

Clerodendrum
Evergreen and deciduous
The shrubby clerodendrums are grown for their ornamental foliage, fragrant flowers produced in summer and early autumn and, in some species, the attractive seedpods and berries.

Clerodendrum trichotomum is best grown with a single stem to help prevent suckering. It can be pruned in spring before the buds break, which will reduce the amount of flowers and fruit, but increase the size of leaves; a good idea if good foliage is required, such as in the variegated cultivar 'Carnival'.

C. bungei may die back in winter and so should be hard pruned in spring at bud break. Where growth is retained through winter, cut back to a framework of branches 60–90cm (2–3ft) from ground level.

Colutea
Bladder senna
Deciduous
This shrub produces yellow, pea-like flowers in summer on the current year's growth, followed by inflated seedpods.

It needs little or no annual pruning other than removing dead or diseased stems, thinning out congested growth and shortening long, wayward growth in spring.

Colutea responds well to hard pruning, and if necessary, you can cut back the branches to within a few buds of their base.

Convolvulus cneorum
Evergreen
This evergreen produces silvery-grey foliage, and in spring and summer – or sometimes through autumn – white flowers that have a yellow centre and are pink in bud.

Plants do not need regular pruning, but over-long and wayward shoots can be cut back to their base or a healthy sideshoot in early spring before the buds begin to break. Shoots affected by winter dieback can be cut out at the same time.

C. cneorum does not respond well to hard pruning, and old or neglected plants should be replaced.

Cordyline
See palms and palm-like plants on page 106.

Cornus
Dogwood, Cornelian cherry
Deciduous
The dogwoods are mainly grown for their colourful winter stems, but they also produce flowers in late spring, followed by white or pale blue fruit. Some cultivars have attractive, variegated foliage. All pruning is carried out in early spring, before the buds break.

If growing dogwoods for their flowers, fruit and foliage, don't prune them, apart from restricting their spread when one in three or four stems can be removed each year. Neglected plants can be renovated by cutting out old wood at the centre of the plant.

When growing for their colourful stems, the best colour always comes from young stems, so annual pruning is needed. Don't prune in the first year after planting, but in the second year cut back all stems to 5cm (2in) from the ground. In subsequent years, cut back all the stems to within two or three buds of the previous year's growth.

To get the best of both worlds, cut back one-third of the stems each year, removing the oldest and the thickest ones. Alternatively, hard prune every two or three years. Annual pruning is not ideal for the less vigorous *C. sanguinea*, so remove one stem in three annually, or hard prune to ground level every other year

The Cornelian cherry (*C. mas*) is grown for its yellow flowers that appear in winter or early spring, followed by excellent autumn leaf colours and bright red fruit. Any pruning is carried out in early summer, but keep this to a minimum by just thinning out unwanted stems. You can rejuvenate overgrown or neglected plants by cutting back stems to two or three buds.

For pruning the tree cornus, *see* page 94.

Coronilla
Evergreen and deciduous

These plants are grown for their ornamental, often blue-green foliage and yellow spring flowers; some will flower from autumn to spring, but they need a protected site.

Little pruning is needed apart from removing dead and old, unattractive growth at the base of the plant in spring after flowering. Plants don't respond well to hard pruning.

Corylopsis
Winter hazel
Deciduous

Corylopsis is grown for its hazel-like catkins produced in winter and early spring on the previous year's growth.

It doesn't need regular pruning, apart from removing dead growth; indeed, pruning can spoil its otherwise attractive shape. Long and wayward branches can be cut back to their base, if absolutely necessary, after flowering.

Corylus
Hazel
Deciduous

Hazels are grown for their attractive foliage, their catkins in late winter and spring, and their nuts. Some cultivars, such as *C. avellana* 'Contorta', are also grown for their twisted stems.

The shrubby hazels are grown as multi-stemmed bushes, and to ensure there is a good balance of new and mature growth, one or two of the oldest stems should be removed at ground level in late winter. Plants can also be coppiced.

To renovate neglected plants, cut back all stems to ground level in late winter.

For pruning *Corylus colurna*, *see* page 94; for pruning for nuts, *see* page 130.

Cotinus coggygria 'Golden Spirit'. *(Photo: Geoff Hodge)*

Cotinus

Smoke bush
Deciduous

This large shrub is grown for its smoke-like plumes of summer flowers and its attractive, ornamental foliage, which can produce excellent autumn colours. How you prune it depends on which attribute you wish to encourage; all pruning should be done in late winter or early spring before growth starts.

During the first spring after planting, cut back growth made the previous year by about one-third to help create a well branched shrub.

The flowers are produced on two- to three-year-old wood, and usually only during hot summers. To encourage flowers, keep pruning to a minimum, just thin out overcrowded shoots.

If you want to encourage foliage displays, cut back the stems by half to three-quarters; the harder you prune, the better the foliage. Don't prune harder than this, as plants will produce shoots that are not very vigorous.

For the best of both worlds, cut out one stem in three each spring, starting with the oldest.

Cotoneaster

Evergreen and deciduous

Cotoneasters are grown for their various habits – from ground cover to small trees – for the masses of summer flowers, the autumn foliage in the deciduous types, and the autumn berries.

They only need minimal pruning to keep them within bounds, to thin out unwanted growth and remove any damaged shoots. Deciduous forms can be pruned from winter to mid-spring, evergreens in spring.

For pruning hedges, *see* page 109.

Cytisus

Broom
Deciduous

These brooms are fast-growing but short-lived shrubs that flower in spring on growth produced the previous year. After planting, lightly cut back or pinch out the growing tips to encourage a bushy habit.

You can extend their life and flowering performance by annual pruning, removing the faded flowers to prevent seed production. Pruning also encourages new growth for the following year's flowers.

Prune established plants immediately after flowering in early to mid-summer. Cut out the spent flowers, reducing the flowering stems by two-thirds of the previous year's growth.

Avoid cutting back too hard as new shoots will not be produced when plants are cut back into old wood. Old or overgrown plants are best replaced.

Daboecia

Heath
Evergreen

Dwarf, low-growing plants grown for ground cover and which are covered in flowers from summer to autumn, depending on the cultivar.

Clip back the plants after flowering to remove all the spent flowers and a small amount of leafy growth below them.

Straggly and neglected plants can be cut back harder, but not into very old wood.

Danae

Alexandrian laurel
Evergreen

This suckering shrub is grown for its arching stems, much loved by flower arrangers, and its orange-red autumn berries.

In late spring, prune unwanted stems to ground level. To restrict plants that have suckered and spread too far, cut off the suckers with a spade. Old, neglected plants can be renovated by cutting back all the stems to ground level.

Daphne

Evergreen/deciduous

Daphnes require minimal pruning and are best left unpruned as they can suffer from dieback; completely remove any dieback as soon as it is seen. Pruning should only be to remove damaged, diseased or wayward growth; this is carried out in early spring or immediately after flowering. *Daphne odora* and *D. cneorum* will tolerate light trimming to maintain a compact, symmetrical habit.

Desfontainea spinosa
Evergreen

This shrub produces holly-like leaves and tubular red and yellow flowers from summer to autumn.

Pruning should be kept to a minimum, by just removing dead, damaged and a few unwanted branches in spring.

Deutzia × *hybrida* 'Mont Rose'. *(Photo: Tim Sandall)*

Deutzia
Deciduous

Deutzia is grown for its showy summer flowers produced on new shoots from the previous year's growth.

After planting, tip back the young shoots to encourage bushy growth. All further pruning is carried out after flowering. Prune to young shoots below the growth that has flowered. As plants get older, remove some of the oldest branches to ground level or to a strong, low-growing shoot.

Plants can be renovated by cutting back old stems to ground level and shortening the others to low sideshoots; they will take a couple of years to flower well.

Dipelta
Deciduous

This shrub is grown for its showy summer flowers and the peeling bark that appears on mature plants.

It should be pruned after flowering, cutting back one in five of the oldest stems to ground level. Any stems showing signs of dieback should also be cut out.

Elaeagnus
Oleaster
Evergreen and deciduous

Elaeagnus are grown for their small, but highly scented summer or autumn flowers and their attractive foliage. Several variegated evergreen forms are available.

They do not need regular/annual pruning as they naturally produce well-shaped plants. Wayward branches or unrequired growth should be removed in summer – after flowering for the deciduous species, and late summer for the evergreen ones.

They tolerate hard pruning, and can be pruned back into old wood if needed.

For pruning hedges, *see* page 109.

Enkianthus
Pagoda bush
Deciduous

Enkianthus is grown for its bell-shaped spring flowers, autumn leaf colour and reddish young stems.

No regular pruning is needed. Plants can be deadheaded after flowering, and crowded branches can be thinned out at the same time.

Leggy and overgrown plants respond well to hard pruning after flowering.

Erica
Heather
Evergreen

Dwarf, low-growing plants grown for ground cover that are covered in flowers from late autumn to spring, depending on the cultivar.

They should be pruned annually after flowering to keep them compact and to ensure long life and long flowering. Simply shear off all the old flowering stems, together with some of the leafy growth below. Never cut back into old wood as plants rarely recover.

Straggly and neglected plants can be cut back harder, but not into very old wood.

Erica arborea, the tree heather, should be cut back by up to two-thirds in the first two or three years to promote bushy growth. Afterwards, plants need little pruning, but overlong shoots can be cut back if needed. Old, neglected plants can be cut back hard into old wood, but total regeneration is best done over two years.

Escallonia
Evergreen

These shrubs produce their summer or early autumn flowers on the previous year's growth.

During the first few years, prune lightly to encourage bushy growth. After that, no regular pruning is needed, but cut back any shoots that spoil the symmetry of the shrubs. Pruning is carried out after flowering, although if they finish flowering late in the year it may be better to leave pruning until the following spring. During very harsh winter weather they may suffer some dieback, which should be pruned out.

Old, neglected plants can be renovated by hard pruning in mid- to late spring.

For pruning hedges, *see* page 109.

Euonymus
Evergreen and deciduous

The deciduous forms are grown for their autumn leaf colour and fruit, while the evergreens are grown for their ornamental foliage. Neither needs very much in the way of formative pruning.

Prune deciduous forms in late winter or early spring to thin out congested stems, cutting out the older ones to ground level to help open up the centre.

The evergreens are pruned in mid- to late spring simply to remove unwanted growth. Forms of *E. fortunei* are sometimes grown as wall shrubs, but need little pruning apart from cutting out old, unproductive growth.

For pruning hedges, *see* page 109.

Exochorda
Deciduous

This plant has a graceful, arching habit and produces white flowers in late spring and early summer on the previous year's growth.

Established plants can be pruned annually after flowering to remove weak growth and reduce over-crowding. Cut out one in three of the oldest stems

Exochorda × macrantha 'The Bride'.
(Photo: Tim Sandall)

to ground level, and remove any other stems that are causing overcrowding.

Neglected plants can be renovated by removing all old stems after flowering.

× *Fatshedera lizei*
Evergreen

This evergreen is grown for its handsome foliage. It has a sprawling habit and is often used as ground cover, but may also be trained up a wall.

Little or no pruning is needed apart from removing dead, damaged or unwanted growth; this is best done in spring.

Fatsia japonica
False castor oil plant
Evergreen

Fatsia is grown for its handsome, hand-shaped foliage and also for its clusters of white flowers in autumn.

It needs little in the way of pruning, although winter-damaged shoots and leaves should be removed in late spring. Sparse and unwanted branches are best removed completely to ground level in spring.

Old, neglected plants usually respond well to having old stems cut back hard to ground level.

Forsythia
Deciduous

Forsythias provide a splash of spring colour, the plants covered in yellow flowers, produced mostly on mature, but not very old wood. Pruning should be carried out after flowering.

Keep pruning to a minimum during the first two or three years after planting. Once established, however, older plants that are not pruned become woody at the base and produce fewer flowers: to avoid this, prune annually by thinning out over-crowded stems at the centre of the plant, and cutting out one in three of the main stems at the base, starting with the oldest.

Neglected plants can be rejuvenated by cutting back all flowered shoots to a strong bud near to the base of the shrub. This is best staggered over two years.

For pruning *F. suspensa* as a wall shrub, *see* page 69.

Fothergilla
Deciduous

An attractive large shrub grown for its spring flowers and fabulous autumn leaf colouring.

Little or no annual pruning is needed, other than the removal of dead or diseased stems and thinning out any congested growth as the flowers fade and before the leaves open. Always cut back to a healthy sideshoot lower down.

Fuchsia
Deciduous

Fuchsias produce a profusion of flowers from summer right through until the first frosts on the current year's growth.

Pinch out the tips of young plants to encourage bushy growth. In spring, if the top growth has been killed, cut plants back to near ground level, taking care not to damage emerging shoots. In mild areas, top growth may survive, in which case remove any dead growth and thin out congested stems. Plants can also be kept within bounds by cutting back main stems to healthy sideshoots lower down.

For pruning bedding fuchsias, *see* page 23.

Fuchsia magellanica. (Photo: Geoff Hodge)

Gaultheria
Evergreen

Gaultheria now includes all plants previously listed as *Pernettya* as well as *x Gaulnettya*. They are grown for their ornamental foliage and attractive winter berries that follow the bell-shaped flowers produced in May.

Little pruning is needed, although plants can be trimmed back after flowering in spring, and suckers can be removed to restrict their spread.

Genista
Broom
Deciduous

Genistas produce their colourful, pea-like flowers in spring or summer on growth that is two years old.

Cut back after flowering to keep the plants bushy and compact, removing the growth that has flowered.

Most brooms do not produce new growth if they are cut back hard into old, brown wood, and neglected plants are best replaced.

Griselinia
Evergreen

Griselinia is grown for its glossy, evergreen foliage. Little or no regular pruning is needed, but being susceptible to frost it may need to have any dead or damaged growth removed in spring.

For pruning hedges, *see* page 00.

× Halimiocistus and Halimium
Evergreen

Colourful small shrubs, often used for ground cover, covered in individually short-lived flowers in summer.

After planting, plants can be pruned to encourage bushiness; certainly any tall shoots are best cut back by up to two-thirds to sideshoots.

Established plants need little or no pruning, but dead and damaged shoots can be removed after flowering, together with any wayward growth.

Old, neglected plants do not respond well to being cut back hard.

Hamamelis
Witch hazel
Deciduous

Witch hazels are grown for their highly scented winter flowers and highly colourful autumn leaf colours.

Keep pruning to a minimum, apart from the removal of dead or diseased branches, and others to maintain the shape; pruning should be carried out after flowering. Always cut back to a healthy sideshoot lower down the stem.

Hebe
Evergreen

All hebes are grown for their ornamental foliage, and the majority for their attractive flowers.

Hebes grown for their foliage rather than their flowers, such as *H. cupressoides* and *H. ochracea*, can be pruned in spring to achieve a compact and neat habit; shears can be used as opposed to secateurs. Neglected plants can be cut back hard since new shoots will be readily produced from near to the base.

Hebes grown for their flowers and foliage should only be pruned in mid- to late spring, as new growth starts, to remove frost-damaged, dead or

Helianthemum 'Butter and Eggs'. *(Photo: Tim Sandall)*

diseased growth. Plants can be hard pruned if they become too top heavy, but depending on their age and health, they may die back and need replacing.

Helianthemum
Rock rose
Evergreen

Rock roses are low-growing, prostrate shrubs covered in flowers in summer.

Young plants should be pinched back after planting to encourage bushy growth.

Established plants should be lightly pruned after flowering to remove flowering stems and so prevent the build up of old, unproductive stems.

Old, neglected plants don't respond well to hard pruning and are best replaced.

Helichrysum italicum
Curry plant
Evergreen

The curry plant is grown for its aromatic, silvery-grey foliage and yellow summer flowers.

In spring remove winter-damaged stems and cut back leggy shoots to just above old wood.

Old, neglected plants usually respond well to hard pruning in late spring.

Hibiscus

Deciduous

The hardy, shrubby hibiscus is grown for its large, showy summer flowers produced on the current year's growth.

Young plants should be cut back by half to two-thirds after planting to encourage bushy growth. Pruning established plants is best kept to a minimum, but shoots showing signs of dieback should be removed in late spring. Lopsided and badly shaped plants can have these branches removed.

Hippophae rhamnoides

Sea buckthorn

Deciduous

Hippophae rhamnoides is a suckering shrub grown for its willow-like silvery leaves and orange berries, which are produced on female plants.

Little pruning is needed, apart from thinning out unwanted stems to ground level in summer if plants become too thick, and to remove unwanted suckers from the periphery of the plant.

Plants respond well to hard pruning, but this often results in excess sucker production, too.

For pruning hedges, *see* page 109.

Hydrangea

Deciduous

There are several groups of hydrangea, but they all flower in late summer or autumn. They respond well to pruning, providing it is done at the right time.

Neglected plants usually respond well to hard pruning in mid- to late spring to renovate them.

Lacecaps and mopheads produce their growth on the previous year's growth, the other hydrangeas on the current year's growth.

Mopheads, *H. serrata*

Dead flower heads of mophead hydrangeas can be removed after flowering, but it is better to leave them on the plant over winter as they provide some frost protection for the tender growth buds below. Instead, remove the dead flower heads in early spring, cutting back to the first strong, healthy pair of buds.

If there is any frost damage, prune back damaged shoots to just above the first undamaged pair of buds on live, healthy wood. Also remove any weak, straggly stems.

Lacecaps

Lacecaps are hardier and need less pruning, although faded flower heads can be cut back to the second pair of leaves below the head in spring.

Neglected or old plants can be hard pruned to the ground in spring, but there will be no flowers that year.

Other hydrangeas

H. arborescens, H. paniculata

Pruning isn't necessary, but plants tend to flower better if pruned annually in spring to a low framework between 30–60cm (1–2ft) high. In the first spring after planting, cut back all new growth to within 5cm (2in) of the old wood. Then every year cut back all the previous year's growth to the lowest pair of buds where it joins the main framework of branches. If this is too severe, reduce by about half instead.

Old and neglected plants usually respond well if pruned back hard to the main framework.

H. aspera, H. quercifolia, H. sargentiana, H. villosa

These need minimal pruning; any work should be carried out in spring.

For pruning climbing hydrangeas, *see* page 71.

Hypericum

Evergreen and deciduous

Hypericums produce bright yellow, saucer-shaped flowers in summer and autumn on the current year's growth. Pruning is carried out in spring.

For the shrubby hypericums, remove old, damaged and thin shoots and reduce the remaining stems to within 5–10cm (2–4in) from the ground or to strong sideshoots; this will help keep plants compact and bushy.

Hypericum androsaemum and *H.* × *inodorum* are best pruned only every two or three years rather than annually. *H. calycinum* (rose of Sharon) can have all the previous year's growth cut back with shears to within a few centimetres (inches) of ground level.

Ilex × altaclarensis 'Golden King'. *(Photo: Tim Sandall)*

Ilex
Holly
Evergreen

Most hollies are trees and are covered in the tree section, but there are several shrubby species, too; these include *I. crenata*, *I. x meservae*, *I. opaca* and *I. verticillata*.

They need little regular or maintenance pruning, but any that is needed should be carried out in late summer.

For pruning hedges *see* page 109.

Indigofera
Indigo
Deciduous

This multi-stemmed shrub produces its pea-like flowers in summer and early autumn on the current year's growth.

In warm areas little or no annual pruning is needed. In colder regions remove weak, frosted, damaged or diseased stems and thin out congested growth near to ground level in mid-spring.

Neglected plants will respond well to hard pruning and so can have all stems cut back to near ground level. If this is too drastic, cut out one in three stems, beginning with the oldest; vigorous new growth will result.

Jasminum humile, J. parkeri
Evergreen and deciduous

These shrubby jasmines produce their yellow flowers in summer at the end of shoots produced the previous year.

Don't prune during the first few years after planting. Once established, remove one or two of the old stems after flowering to prevent the build-up of old, unproductive stems. Every few years, prune out one in three stems, starting with the oldest.

For pruning climbing and wall shrub jasmines, *see* page 71.

Kalmia
Calico bush
Evergreen

Kalmias produce glossy foliage and large clusters of flowers in summer.

They need very little pruning, but deadheading is usually worthwhile after flowering if it is achievable.

Overgrown, tall and neglected plants can be hard pruned in mid-spring or after flowering, but extensive hard pruning should be carried out over three to five years.

Kerria
Jew's mallow
Deciduous

This is a suckering shrub producing its yellow flowers in spring on the previous year's growth.

Kolkwitzia amabilis 'Pink Cloud'. *(Photo: Tim Sandall)*

Once established the plant can become very congested, and flowering becomes reduced. After flowering, prune out the flowered stems to ground level or strong sideshoots. Cutting stems back to different levels produces a plant that flowers at different heights.

To restrict plants that have suckered and spread too far, cut off the suckers with a spade. Old, neglected plants can be renovated by cutting back all the stems to ground level.

Kolkwitzia
Beauty bush
Deciduous
The beauty bush produces showy flowers in late spring or early summer on two-year-old wood; it also produces peeling bark, which is attractive in winter.

Allow young plants to develop with little or no thinning. Established plants sucker freely and can be pruned after flowering to remove one in three of the oldest stems. Either cut these out at ground level or to a low sideshoot.

To renovate old and neglected plants cut out old stems to ground level, but always leave between five and seven young stems.

Lavandula
Lavender
Evergreen
Lavenders produce their fragrant flowers in summer on the current year's growth.

Lavatera × clementii 'Barnsley'. *(Photo: Tim Sandall)*

Regular, annual pruning is necessary to keep plants compact and flowering well, otherwise they become leggy and sparse.

Prune newly planted lavender by up to one-third to encourage bushy growth.

The hardier lavenders (*L. angustifolia*) can be pruned after flowering in warm climates, but in cooler regions only deadhead in autumn to tidy up plants, leaving the main pruning until spring. Remove flower stalks and about 2.5–5cm (1–2in) of the growth, making sure that some green growth remains.

L. dentata, *L. × intermedia* and *L. stoechas* are not as hardy and are best pruned in spring.

Lavender does not shoot readily from old wood – it usually dies if pruned hard – and neglected specimens are best replaced.

For pruning hedges, *see* page 109.

Lavatera
Tree mallow
Deciduous
This vigorous shrub produces masses of flowers over a long period from summer to autumn on the current year's growth. Older wood is not very strong and is prone to cracking or snapping, so cut back plants in early autumn by one-third to prevent wind rock and stem damage.

In spring after the risk of severe frosts has passed and the buds are beginning to break, cut stems back hard to between 15–30cm (6–12in) from ground level to form a stubby framework, or to within a few buds of the previous year's growth. Any damaged and weak growth can also be removed during the growing season.

Plants are not long lived, and old, neglected plants do not respond well to very hard pruning.

Leonotis leonurus
Lion's ear
Evergreen
This subshrub is grown for its aromatic foliage and orange-red flowers produced in summer and autumn on the current year's growth. It is not fully hardy.

After planting in spring, tip-prune plants to encourage bushy growth. In subsequent years cut back all growth to 10–15cm (4–6in) from ground level in spring after the danger of frosts. Old plants can be renovated in the same way.

Leptospermum

Tea tree
Evergreen

Leptospermums are grown for their glossy, often aromatic foliage and masses of small, colourful flowers. They are not completely hardy.

After planting, tip-prune shoots to ensure a bushy habit. In subsequent years trim shoots lightly in spring to prevent leggy growth. Plants do not shoot from old growth, so avoid cutting into old wood; neglected plants are best replaced.

Lespedeza

Bush clover
Deciduous

Lespedeza produces its pea-like flowers in late summer and autumn on the current year's growth.

Little pruning is needed, but plants are usually killed down to ground level in winter by severe weather. After the fear of frost has passed, cut down all dead stems to ground level or healthy growth.

Leucothoe

Evergreen

Leucothoe is grown for its attractive leathery foliage. It needs minimal pruning, although one or two of the oldest stems can be cut down to their base in late spring if needed.

Leycesteria

Himalayan honeysuckle, pheasant berry
Deciduous

Leycesteria is grown for its maroon and white pendant flowers and red-purple fruit; new stems can grow and flower in the same year. The bamboo-like stems are also attractive during the winter.

It produces thick clumps of stems, which should be thinned out annually in spring, cutting weak, old and damaged stems to ground level. If left unpruned, plants soon become congested.

Neglected and old specimens can be renovated by cutting back all stems to within 5cm (2in) of the ground.

Leycesteria formosa 'Golden Lanterns Notbruce'. *(Photo: Geoff Hodge)*

Ligustrum

Privet
Evergreen and deciduous

Privets are grown for their ornamental summer flowers and foliage. Although privet is usually thought of as a hedging plant, there are several that are ornamental enough to be grown as specimens – this includes *L. japonicum*, *L. lucidum* and variegated cultivars of common privet *L. ovalifolium*.

No pruning is needed at planting, and keep subsequent pruning to a minimum, just to tidy up plants and remove unwanted growth in spring.

For pruning hedges, *see* page 109.

Lonicera

Shrubby honeysuckle
Evergreen and deciduous

The shrubby honeysuckles includes a number of different species, either grown for their evergreen foliage, or their summer or winter flowers. The blooms of the winter-flowering species are highly scented. Pruning depends on why the plant is grown and, if a flowering species, the time of flowering.

Lonicera nitida is an evergreen grown for its foliage, especially the golden-leaved cultivar 'Baggesen's Gold'; it does produce small, creamy-white flowers. Plants can be trimmed up to three times a year between mid- to late spring and autumn to keep them compact and bushy. *L. pileata* is similar but needs minimal pruning.

L. tatarica and *L. korolkowii* produce summer flowers on the previous year's growth, often followed by colourful berries. *L. fragrantissima* and *L. × purpusii* are winter-flowering species. Both types should be pruned after flowering, removing old and weak stems to their base, and shortening up to one in three of the remaining shoots to help keep them compact and bushy.

All types can be renovated by pruning back to a low framework of branches or to within 15cm (6in) of the ground in early spring.

For pruning climbing honeysuckles, *see* page 72; for pruning hedges, *see* page 109.

Lupinus arboreus
Tree lupin
Evergreen

Tree lupins are grown for their long, stately flower spikes in summer.

They need little in the way of pruning, but in spring you can shorten some of the longest shoots to reduce the plant's size and cut out some of the oldest and weakest growth to help keep the plant in good health and flowering well. Cut off the seedheads after flowering, unless you want to keep the seed.

Magnolia
Deciduous

These large shrubs are grown for their big, showy flowers produced in spring or early summer.

Established magnolias usually do not need regular pruning – and they don't usually respond well to pruning. But where damaged branches or overgrown plants need work, this should be carried out when the tree is in full leaf, usually during mid-

summer. In spring and early summer the wounds will bleed, and pruning in the dormant season often leads to dieback.

Heavy flowering and seed production can reduce the plant's vigour – especially small plants – so try and deadhead if possible.

Plants may not respond well to hard pruning, but overgrown and badly shaped plants can usually be renovated by hard pruning, but this is best staged over three years. Select the highest or widest branches to remove, which will reduce the overall height and spread. Taking out whole branches or side branches helps maintain their graceful shape.

For pruning tree magnolias, see page 98; for pruning *Magnolia grandiflora* as a wall shrub, *see* page 72.

Mahonia japonica. (Photo: Tim Sandall)

Mahonia
Evergreen

Mahonias produce their scented winter flowers on growth produced the previous year, and so are pruned in spring after flowering.

New plants can be encouraged to produce a branching, attractive habit by cutting out the growing tips after flowering; remove the top rosette of leaves along with the spent flower heads.

No regular pruning is needed, but established plants can be kept within bounds and flowering well by pruning out one in three stems, starting with the oldest.

Low-growing *M. aquifolium* used as ground cover can be cut back hard each year during late spring.

Neglected mahonias usually respond – although slowly – to severe pruning, cutting back to a framework 30–60cm (1–2ft) above ground level.

Melianthus major

Honey bush
Evergreen
This evergreen, grown for its attractive, ornamental foliage, is not completely hardy. In cold areas the top growth can be killed down to ground level, in which case this needs clearing away in spring. In milder regions, where the top growth remains intact, cut this back during early spring to within two or three buds from the base.

The sap is an irritant, so wear gloves and a long-sleeved shirt to protect hands and arms.

Nandina domestica

Heavenly bamboo, sacred bamboo
Evergreen
Nandina produces white flowers in summer followed, in warm summers, by red berries in autumn. Some forms also produce excellent autumn leaf colour.

On planting, spindly plants can be cut back to promote bushy growth. Established plants need little pruning, apart from keeping the plant tidy.

Old and neglected plants can be renovated by cutting back the old stems to just above ground level.

Olearia

Daisy bush
Evergreen
Olearias are grown for their attractive foliage and white, daisy-like flowers that are produced in either spring or summer.

After planting, shorten long shoots to encourage a bushy habit.

Once established, keep pruning to a minimum, apart from removing damaged, especially winter-damaged, growth. To keep plants within bounds, prune stems by one-third to half. All types are pruned in spring – the summer-flowering species, such as *O.* × *haastii* and *O. macrodonta*, once new growth begins, and those that flower in spring, such as *O. phlogopappa* and *O.* × *scilloniensis*, after flowering.

Olearias usually respond well to hard pruning and neglected specimens can be renovated in mid- to late spring.

For pruning hedges, *see* page 109.

Osmanthus × burkwoodii. (Photo: Tim Sandall)

Osmanthus

Evergreen
Osmanthus is grown for its ornamental foliage and small, fragrant flowers produced in either spring or summer.

Once established, prune to remove winter-damaged growth and to keep plants within bounds by cutting back overlong shoots. All types are pruned in spring – the summer-flowering ones once new growth begins, and those that flower in spring after flowering.

Osmanthus usually respond well to hard pruning, and neglected specimens can be renovated in mid- to late spring.

For pruning hedges, *see* page 109.

Ozothamnus

Evergreen

Ozothamnus is grown for its ornamental foliage. It needs little pruning, apart from removing damaged growth in spring. It tolerates hard pruning, so neglected plants can be cut back hard.

Pachysandra

Evergreen

A spreading plant that is ideal for ground cover. It produces small flowers in early spring.

It needs little pruning, apart from removing unwanted growth after flowering. Should it become bare and woody, the stems can be cut back to 5–7.5cm (2–3in) from ground level in late spring.

Paeonia

Tree peony
Deciduous

Tree peonies produce large, blousy flowers in summer.

They need little pruning, but you should remove the faded flowers when they have finished or, if you want seeds, after the seeds have been gathered in autumn. It is also worth removing some of the very old, leggy stems of mature plants by cutting them back to ground level in summer.

Penstemon

Evergreen

Penstemons are grown for their masses of summer flowers, often appearing for months on end until the first frosts.

The dwarf and prostrate species, often used in rock gardens, need minimal pruning, but can be sheared over. The taller border types should be pruned annually, especially to enhance the upright growth habit. Pruning should be carried out in spring after the danger of severe frosts.

Border types should have winter damage removed by cutting stems back hard. You can also prune again after flowering by cutting back stems by half to prevent seed production and encourage further flushes of flowers.

Old plants can be renovated by cutting back all the stems hard; however, depending on their age and health, they may not survive such severe pruning.

Perovskia

Russian sage
Deciduous

Russian sage is grown for its aromatic grey-green foliage and spikes of blue flowers in late summer and early autumn, produced at the ends of the current year's growth. Top growth usually dies back in winter, and new shoots are produced from the base in spring.

Plants should be pruned annually in spring as new growth is appearing. Cut back all the previous year's growth to within 5–10cm (2–4in) of ground level in the first few years, and then to a framework of old wood that develops in subsequent years.

Old and neglected plants can be renovated by cutting back hard to the framework of old wood.

Philadelphus 'Belle Etoile'. *(Photo: Geoff Hodge)*

Philadelphus

Orange blossom
Deciduous

Philadelphus are grown for their large, highly fragrant white flowers in summer, produced on the previous year's growth. *P. coronarius* 'Aureus' and *P. coronarius* 'Variegatus' produce smaller flowers, but these are complimented by their attractive coloured foliage.

Plants should be pruned immediately after flowering in summer. They produce new growth from the ground that can, in time, become very crowded, and results in poor flowering. As a result, once established, prune out one in four of the oldest stems annually, by removing them at ground level or to a low-growing sideshoot.

Cultivars grown for their foliage can either be treated in the same way or, for the best leaf colour effect, trimmed over lightly in late spring to remove the flower buds. Or, for a bit of both, try both pruning regimes – cutting back old wood on half the plant, and trimming the other half lightly.

P. microphyllus is a smaller shrub that needs little pruning, but excessive and congested growth can be removed after flowering.

All plants can be renovated by cutting back hard in late winter or early spring.

Phlomis
Evergreen
These shrubs and subshrubs are grown for their mainly grey-green, sage-like foliage and yellow or lilac-pink flowers. Although they are mostly hardy, they may suffer from frost and cold damage. Luckily they usually reshoot from the base.

After planting remove any weak growth, and shorten overlong and straggly stems. After that, established plants don't need regular pruning, apart from removing winter-damaged and long, leggy or wayward stems, by cutting back to a healthy bud or shoot. Old and weak stems should be completely removed. All pruning is done in spring when the plant is actively growing.

Neglected plants can be renovated by cutting back hard to within 7.5–15cm (3–6in) of the ground or, for older plants, a higher framework of branches. Hard pruning may kill very old and unhealthy plants, but is worth trying; otherwise replace the plant with a new one.

Phormium
See palms and palm-like plants on pages 106–107.

Photinia
Evergreen and deciduous
Photinia now includes plants previously listed as *Stranvaesia* and × *Stranvinia*.

They are grown for their white flowers in spring or summer, the glossy, brightly coloured foliage of the evergreen species and fruits, and the autumn foliage colour of the deciduous types. They do not need regular pruning, although the evergreen species are often used for hedging, which will need annual tidying up and shaping.

The evergreens can have shoots cut back by up to 15cm (6in) in spring to encourage the brightly coloured young foliage. The deciduous species can have overcrowded growth removed in winter.

Plants can be renovated by cutting back hard into old wood, or by cutting back to a low framework of branches.

For pruning hedges, *see* page 109.

Phygelius
Cape figwort
Evergreen, semi-evergreen
Phygelius produce their tubular flowers from summer to autumn on the current year's growth.

On planting, plants can be cut back to produce bushy growth. In cold regions, plants may be killed back by cold weather and frost, in which case they should be pruned back to buds on live growth, or if needed, to the base of the plant. This should be done in spring after the danger of frosts has passed. In milder climates plants benefit from light pruning in spring.

Plants can be renovated by cutting back all stems to the ground in late spring.

Physocarpus opulifolius
Ninebark
Deciduous
Physocarpus opulifolius is grown for its white or pink summer flowers; some cultivars have attractively coloured leaves – 'Dart's Gold' is golden yellow, and 'Diabolo' is purple.

Plants should be pruned immediately after flowering in summer. They produce new growth from the ground that can, in time, become very crowded and results in poor flowering. As a result, once established, prune out one in four of the oldest stems annually, by removing them at ground level or to a low-growing shoot.

Old and neglected plants can be renovated by cutting back hard in late winter or early spring.

Pieris 'Forest Flame'. *(Photo: Tim Sandall)*

Pieris

Evergreen

Pieris are grown for their glossy foliage that is brightly coloured pink and red when young, and for their lily-of-the-valley flowers in spring.

Plants need little pruning, apart from deadheading after flowering. Frosted and winter-damaged growth can be removed at the same time, as can any uneven, overlong and lopsided growth.

Old and neglected plants can be cut back to a low framework of branches; plants usually respond well to hard pruning in late spring.

For pruning hedges, *see* page 109.

Piptanthus

Deciduous or semi-evergreen

This shrub is grown for its attractive, yellow, pea-like flowers in spring and early summer, as well as its ornamental foliage and stems.

Plants may be damaged by frost and cold weather, so remove damaged growth in spring. Then remove up to one in four of the oldest stems after flowering in summer.

Pittosporum

Evergreen

Pittosporums are mainly grown for their glossy foliage, although they also produce scented flowers in late spring and summer.

Plants need little pruning, although removing winter-damaged growth, some thinning out and trimming can be done in mid-spring when new growth has started.

Old and neglected plants usually recover well if hard pruned in late spring.

For pruning hedges, *see* page 109.

Potentilla

Deciduous

The shrubby potentillas form rounded shrubs covered in flowers in summer, and often into autumn, produced on the current year's growth.

Pruning should be carried annually in spring, as potentillas tend to become twiggy and unkempt if not pruned regularly. Cut back the oldest stems to their base, remove weak, twiggy growth and shorten young, vigorous shoots by up to half. Plants can also be trimmed over after flowering to help keep them tidy.

Old, neglected plants can usually be renovated by cutting back all the shoots to a low framework in spring

For pruning hedges, *see* page 109.

Prunus

Evergreen and deciduous
Cherry, cherry laurel

The deciduous species are grown for their spring flowers, produced on the previous year's growth, and sometimes their excellent autumn leaf tints, and the evergreens for their large, leathery leaves and fragrant spring or summer flowers.

Pruning is best kept to a minimum – apart from *P. glandulosa* and *P. sinensis* and those used as hedging plants – and carried out in late spring for deciduous species and late spring or early summer for evergreens; autumn and winter pruning must be avoided to prevent problems from diseases.

Evergreens usually need pruning to shape and to remove wayward growth, cutting back to a sideshoot. *P. glandulosa* and *P. sinensis* need regular pruning to ensure plenty of flowers.

Old and neglected plants may respond well to hard renovation pruning, cutting back to a framework of main branches or even to almost ground level.

For tree *Prunus*, *see* page 100; for fruiting *Prunus*, *see* page 115; for hedges, *see* page 109.

Pyracantha. (Photo: Geoff Hodge)

Pyracantha
Firethorn
Evergreen

Pyracanthas produce good, glossy foliage, are covered with white flowers in summer and colourful berries in autumn and winter.

Plants need little formative pruning or cutting back when established, apart from removing wayward and overlong shoots that spoil the shape in spring.

Plants usually respond well to hard renovation pruning, cutting them back hard to their main stems.

For pruning wall shrubs, *see* page 74; for pruning hedges, *see* page 109.

Rhododendron
Rhododendron, azalea
Evergreen and deciduous

Rhododendrons and azaleas are grown for their attractive shapes and colourful spring flowers, which are produced during the previous summer. The rhododendrons and evergreen azaleas are also grown for their often year-round ornamental foliage, and many of the deciduous azaleas for their colourful autumn foliage tints.

Most *Rhododendron* need little pruning other than the removal of dead and unwanted growth, which should be cut back to a sideshoot or bud. In fact, some of the large-leaved and smooth-barked rhododendrons, such as *R. barbatum*, *R. taliense* and *R. thomsonii*, are shy to break from old growth. Deciduous azaleas may benefit from having very old, unproductive shoots removed.

However, they do respond well to deadheading immediately after flowering, carefully breaking off the old flower head with thumb and forefinger, ensuring no damage to the buds below. Any pruning that is needed is carried out at the same time.

All Rhododendron respond well to hard renovation pruning; all the old stems can be cut back to ground level, or to low-growing buds or shoots after flowering.

Rhus
Sumach
Deciduous

Sumachs can be grown as large shrubs, or trained to have a clear stem to make a small tree. They are mainly grown for their brilliant autumn leaf colour and the large spikes of fruits produced on female plants. Wear gloves and long sleeves when pruning, as the sap can be irritating.

Plants grown as shrubs can be left mainly unpruned, but crowded shoots can be thinned out in early spring. *R. typhina* 'Dissecta' and other similar cultivars are best hard pruned annually or every other year to enhance their cut or fern-like foliage. You can either cut back plants to 15cm (6in) from ground level, or to a low framework of woody stems.

To grow as a standard tree, train a main stem upwards and remove other stems and sideshoots to produce a clear stem to about 1.2m (4ft) high.

Ribes sanguineum 'Pulborough Scarlet'.
(Photo: Tim Sandall)

Plants can be renovated by cutting them back to almost ground level. This will result in numerous new shoots, which will subsequently need thinning out.

Ribes

Flowering currant
Deciduous
Flowering currants produce masses of flowers in spring on the previous year's growth.
Unpruned plants produce lots of old wood, and flowering then declines. Plants should therefore be pruned annually after flowering to keep them vigorous and free flowering. Remove one in three or four stems, starting with the oldest.

Neglected and overgrown shrubs can be rejuvenated by cutting back all stems to just above ground level; this is best done in late winter.

For pruning hedges, *see* page 109.

Romneya

Tree poppy
Deciduous
The tree poppy produces white flowers at the ends of stems from mid-summer to mid-autumn.

Plants may be killed back to ground level in cold winters, in which case all damaged growth should be cut back to live growth or ground level in spring. In warmer areas, where winter damage doesn't occur, up to half of the stems should be cut back near to ground level.

Rosmarinus officinalis

Rosemary
Evergreen
Rosemary produces aromatic, grey-green foliage and blue flowers in spring on the previous year's growth.

Established plants need little or no pruning, except to remove wayward and overlong shoots in early summer after flowering. Any winter dieback can be removed in late spring. Plants can also be reshaped at this time if needed.

Healthy plants can be renovated by cutting back all the stems by up to half in late spring. Old and neglected plants are best replaced as they rarely reshoot well from old wood.

For pruning hedges, *see* page 109.

Rubus

Ornamental bramble
Deciduous
Although most ornamental brambles are grown for their ornamental coloured stems in winter, they all flower, and one or two types are grown mainly for their floral displays.

Those grown for their stems should have the flowered growth removed to ground level in summer after flowering.

Those grown for their flowers are pruned less severely, with just one in three or four of the oldest stems being cut back to ground level after flowering. The remaining stems can be cut back by about one-third to a vigorous shoot to help maintain the shape.

Old plants can be renovated by cutting back all stems to ground level in spring.

For fruiting brambles, *see* page 131.

Ruta graveolens

Rue
Evergreen
Rue is mainly grown for its blue-grey foliage, although it does produce yellow flowers in summer.

Pruning in early spring keeps plants compact and the foliage neat and fresh, but at the expense of the flowers. Cut back all shoots by about half and remove weak stems. If you want to enjoy the flowers, delay pruning until after they fade, and cut back the flowered shoots to within 2.5cm (1in) of old growth.

Old, neglected plants usually respond well to cutting back to within 10–15cm (4–6in) of ground level in spring.

Always wear gloves when pruning to prevent contact with the irritant or toxic sap.

Salix
Willow
Deciduous
There are several shrubby willows that are grown for their catkins and colourful winter stems. Pruning should be carried out in spring, after the catkins have faded in species grown for this attribute.

Those grown for their winter stems should be pruned annually for the same reason, and in the same way, as dogwoods (*see* page 36 for details).

Other willows need lighter, less regular pruning, although established plants can become woody and congested if left unpruned. So prune every other year, removing one in three stems, starting with the oldest.

For pruning tree willows, *see* page 102.

Salvia
Sage
Evergreen
The shrubby salvias are mainly grown for their aromatic, attractive foliage (*S. officinalis*, common sage), although there are several that also produce ornamental summer and autumn flowers, such as *S. microphylla* and *S. greggii*, although these are not as hardy.

During the first spring after planting *S. officinalis*, tip back the stems to encourage bushy growth. Established plants can be kept compact and vigorous by cutting back during mid-spring. This will produce the best foliage displays from cultivars grown for their ornamental foliage. Flowers are best removed in summer, by cutting back to strong growth. Old and neglected plants can be partially renovated by cutting back into old wood, but don't prune too hard

Pruning of the less hardy species is best kept to a minimum – remove any growth that has been killed by winter weather. Tip-pruning of the

Salvia microphylla. (Photo: Tim Sandall)

branches in spring when growth starts will encourage bushy growth, and established plants can be cut back to a woody framework if necessary. Neglected plants may respond to pruning back hard to near ground level.

Sambucus
Elder
Deciduous
Some *Sambucus* are grown for their flowers and berries, while others are mainly grown for their ornamental, often brightly coloured and even finely cut foliage. They all respond well to regular pruning – especially those grown for their foliage. When grown as a multi-stemmed shrub, they can become tall and straggly unless pruned regularly, but some of the taller species can also be grown as single-stemmed trees.

Pruning is carried out in winter when the plants are dormant. Start by removing old and weak shoots, opening up the centre of congested plants, and trimming back young shoots. Then in the second year cut back two-year-old stems to just above ground level, and one-year-old shoots by about half.

Those grown for their ornamental foliage are pruned hard annually, cutting back to ground level or to a low framework of branches. If you want to retain the height, prune back some stems in this way and then cut back the sideshoots on all remaining stems to two or three buds.

Old and neglected plants can be renovated by cutting back to ground level, but if they are very old and weak they may not reshoot.

Santolina
Cotton lavender
Evergreen
Cotton lavender produces aromatic, finely divided grey-green foliage and yellow button-like flowers in summer. Plants need regular pruning, otherwise they can become straggly and bare at the base.

After planting, shorten stems by up to one-third to encourage bushy growth. Thereafter, trim off faded flowers and wayward and overlong shoots annually after flowering. If plants become straggly, hard prune in spring, cutting back most of the previous year's growth.

Neglected plants can be renovated by cutting back hard into old wood, but old and tired plants rarely respond to this treatment and are best replaced.

For pruning hedges, *see* page 109.

Sarcococca
Winter box, Christmas box
Evergreen
The winter box is grown for its shiny evergreen foliage and highly scented winter flowers produced on the previous year's growth.

Little is needed in the way of regular pruning. Plants can be trimmed back, and overlong and wayward stems removed, if necessary, in spring after flowering.

Neglected plants can be renovated by cutting back stems to around 30cm (12in) from ground level in mid-spring.

For pruning hedges, *see* page 109.

Skimmia
Evergreen
Skimmias are grown for their glossy foliage, fragrant spring flowers and, in female forms, long-lasting red fruit.

Skimmias are naturally dense, compact shrubs and need little or no regular pruning. Lopsided growth and wayward stems can be pruned back after flowering, cutting back to well within the bush to hide the cut shoots.

Skimmia × confusa 'Kew Green'. *(Photo: Tim Sandall)*

Neglected plants can be cut back hard in spring, but old plants are best replaced.

Sorbaria
False spiraea
Deciduous
Sorbaria is grown for its cut foliage and white summer flowers.

Prune in winter, completely removing one or two of the oldest stems and cutting back hard the previous year's flowered shoots.

Old plants can be rejuvenated by cutting back all stems close to ground level.

Spartium
Spanish broom
Deciduous
The Spanish broom produces fragrant, yellow flowers in summer and autumn on the current year's growth.

If left unpruned, plants become top heavy and flowering is reduced, so prune in spring when growth starts to keep them compact and long flowering. Encourage new plants to produce a bushy habit by cutting back all new growth by about half during the first two springs after planting. Established shrubs should be pruned every couple of years by cutting back the previous year's growth to within 5cm (2in) of older wood.

Overgrown plants can be hard pruned, but don't always respond well to severe pruning and are best replaced.

Spiraea japonica 'Goldflame'. *(Photo: Tim Sandall)*

Spiraea
Deciduous

Spiraeas are grown for their abundant, attractive flowers produced either in spring on the previous year's growth, or in summer on the current year's growth. Some cultivars of the summer-flowering *S. japonica*, such as 'Goldflame' and 'Gold Mound', are also grown for their colourful foliage; *S. × vanhouttei* 'Pink Ice' is spring-flowering and has variegated foliage.

Spring-flowering species are pruned after flowering. Cut back the flowered stems of young plants to strong buds where new growth is emerging. Once established, cut back one in three or four of the oldest stems to ground level, and shorten the remaining flowered shoots by up to half.

The summer-flowering species are pruned in late winter or early spring. Cut them back to a stubby framework of shoots about 10–15cm (4–6in) from the ground or even harder, 5–7.5cm (2–3in) from ground level.

Old and neglected plants may respond well to hard pruning, but it may be better to leave two or three of the youngest stems unpruned.

For pruning hedges, *see* page 109.

Stachyurus
Deciduous

This is mainly grown for its flowers, produced in spring on buds produced the previous autumn, although *S. chinensis* 'Magpie' is also grown for its variegated foliage.

Stachyurus needs little in the way of regular pruning, but old and thin growth can be cut down to its base, and overlong and wayward stems cut back by up to one-third, in spring after flowering.

Stephanandra
Deciduous

This suckering shrub is mainly grown for its autumn leaf colour and brown stems in winter; the summer flowers are insignificant.

Plants should be thinned in summer after flowering by removing one in three or four of the oldest stems to their base. Some of the remaining flowered stems should also be cut back to strong sideshoots.

Old and neglected plants can be renovated by cutting back all stems to their base in winter or early spring.

Symphoricarpos
Snowberry
Deciduous

The snowberry is a suckering shrub producing summer flowers followed by marble-like berries.

Encourage new plants to produce thick, bushy growth by cutting back to 30cm (12in) after planting. In subsequent years, little or no pruning is necessary other than the removal of any misplaced or old twiggy growth in spring to maintain a permanent framework. If it spreads too far, restrict its growth by chopping away the excess suckers with a spade.

Plants can be renovated by cutting back to near ground level.

For pruning hedges, *see* page 109.

Syringa
Lilac
Deciduous

Lilacs are usually grown as shrubs, but the common lilac (*S. vulgaris*) can also become tree-like with age. They are grown for their fragrant flowers produced in spring and summer on the previous year's growth.

Young plants may need some formative pruning, in summer as the flowers fade, to encourage a

Syringa vulgaris. (Photo: Tim Sandall)

balanced and bushy shape. Thereafter, if it's practical, plants should be carefully deadheaded after flowering; take care not to damage the young shoots, which will carry the following year's flowers. At the same time, thin out weak and spindly shoots and, if space is tight, trim back some of the other stems.

Plants can be renovated by cutting back the main stems to 30–60cm (1–2ft) from ground level, although this is best carried out over two to three years. Plants usually respond by producing lots of new shoots, which generally need to be thinned out; this can delay flowering by a couple of years.

S. × *josiflexa* and *S. yunnanensis* are treated in the same way.

The more bushy lilacs, such as *S. meyeri* and *S. pubescens* subsp. *microphylla* 'Superba', need minimal pruning, but can be cut back and thinned out if necessary after flowering.

Tamarix
Tamarisk
Deciduous or evergreen
Tamarix produce feathery, plume-like foliage and masses of pink flowers.

After planting, cut back all stems by half to encourage a bushy habit; in the following year similar pruning may be needed with plants that still look straggly.

Species such as *T. parviflora* and *T. tentandra* flower in spring and early summer on the previous year's growth and are pruned annually in summer after flowering. *T. pentandra* and *T. ramosissima* flower in late summer on the current year's growth and are pruned annually in early spring. Pruning consists of cutting back flowered growth to strong sideshoots. Late summer-flowering species can also be hard pruned to further encourage flowering and to keep the plants bushy.

For pruning hedges, *see* page 109.

Thymus
Thyme
Evergreen
Thymes are grown for their aromatic foliage and scented summer flowers. They are generally low-growing, ground-cover plants.

Regular pruning or shearing over after flowering will help keep plants neat and tidy, and ensure a steady supply of fresh leaves for use in cooking.

Old plants won't reshoot from old, woody growth, and neglected plants are best replaced.

Ulex
Gorse
Although gorse is virtually leafless, its green stems and spines give it the appearance of being evergreen.

Young plants should be kept bushy by cutting back all stems by a quarter to one-third in spring. Once established, plants can be trimmed over after flowering to keep them compact, and long and wayward stems removed.

Old and neglected plants can be renovated by cutting them back hard to within 15cm (6in) of ground level in spring.

Viburnum
Evergreen and deciduous
The viburnums are a diverse group of shrubs, from low-growing ground cover to tall stately plants. They are grown for their flowers, often highly scented and produced at various times of year, for their berries and, in some deciduous species, their autumn leaf tints. Viburnums rarely need regular annual pruning.

The deciduous autumn- and winter-flowering *Viburnum* × *bodnantense* and *Viburnum farreri* produce their flowers on growth produced the previous summer. Established bushes produce new stems from the base, and can have one in four or five of the oldest, weakest and most unproductive stems removed after flowering in early spring.

The following species are treated in the same way, but are best pruned in late winter: *V. betulifolium*; *V. lantana*; *V. opulus*; *V. rhytidophyllum*.

The evergreen *V. tinus* has a long flowering period – from autumn through to spring – and should be pruned in spring or early summer after flowering. When young, it may need some formative pruning, but once established only prune to maintain the overall shape and height.

V. plicatum flowers in late spring and early summer on the previous year's growth and established plants can be pruned in summer after flowering. Remove old and unproductive growth and anything that spoils the overall shape of the plant.

V. × burkwoodii, *V. × carlcephalum* and *V. carlesii* need minimum pruning, but if required this should be carried out in summer. The ground cover *V. davidii* only needs wayward shoots removing, which will also help to keep it compact.

All plants usually respond to hard renovation pruning carried out in mid- to late spring, although this may spoil the shape of *V. plicatum*.

For pruning *V. tinus* hedges, *see* page 109.

Vinca

Periwinkle

Evergreen

Periwinkle is used as extensive ground cover, its attractive foliage and flowers covering large areas. To prevent the plant from becoming invasive, cut back any unwanted shoots in spring. You can even use shears or a nylon-line trimmer to cut back large areas of ground cover.

Weigela

Deciduous

Weigelas are grown for their late spring or summer flowers produced on the previous year's growth; some also have attractive coloured foliage.

Plants should be pruned annually after flowering to encourage strong new growth for the following year's display. Cut back flowered stems to strong shoots below the flowers. At the same time,

Weigela 'Briant Rubidor' = 'Olympiade'. *(Photo: Tim Sandall)*

if the plant is large enough, cut down one or two old stems to their base, then shorten overlong and wayward growth. Cultivars grown for their foliage will benefit from harder pruning – cut out about three in four of the older stems and shorten the remainder by about two-thirds.

To renovate old plants, cut down all the stems to within 15cm (6in) of ground level, and be prepared to thin out the resulting excess shoots in summer.

Yucca

See palms and palm-like plants on pages 106–107.

BAMBOOS

Bamboos look dramatic in the garden and produce a pleasing sound when the wind rustles their foliage. They do need some basic maintenance, otherwise they can become crowded and untidy and will lose their appealing looks.

In spring remove any weak, dead, damaged or spindly canes from the base of the plant with secateurs, loppers or even a saw. Bamboos are tough plants and can easily inflict scratches and cuts, so wear thick gloves.

Clumps that have become too dense and congested can be thinned out in spring or late summer. Aim to cut out the oldest canes to let light and air through the clump. This then enables young canes to grow unchecked and will result in a more attractive effect, especially with those species that have coloured stems, as the colour is more intense in young canes. Avoid partially shortening canes, as this can look unsightly. Then, without damaging new shoots, clear away any debris at the base.

A few bamboos will flower once the canes are several years old, so it is best to remove the canes before this happens; flowered canes should certainly be completely removed.

To limit the spread of bamboos, you can try cutting through the tough rhizomes and removing portions of the root in spring; these can be replanted elsewhere. However, with vigorous species you may have more success limiting their spread with a physical barrier inserted vertically into the ground.

Dwarf bamboos usually respond well to clipping them down to 10–15cm (4–6in) from ground level in spring with shears or secateurs. This encourages new growth with fresh young foliage.

Pruning Calendar

	spring			summer			autumn			winter		
Abelia			■			■	■					
Acer japonicum, A. palmatum										■	■	■
Amelanchier										■	■	■
Aralia		■	■									
Arbutus		■	■									
Artemisia	■	■										
Aucuba		■										
Berberis			■						■	■	■	■
Brachyglottis (Dunedin Group) 'Sunshine'		■	■									
Buddleja davidii		■										
Buddleja alternifolia				■	■	■						
Buddleja globosa											■	■
Buxus				■	■	■						
Callicarpa	■	■										
Callistemon					■	■	■					
Calluna					■	■	■	■	■			
Camellia		■	■									
Carpenteria					■	■	■					
Caryopteris		■	■									
Ceratostigma		■	■									
Chaenomeles			■	■	■							
Chimonanthus		■										
Choisya		■	■									
Cistus					■	■	■					
Clerodendrum	■	■										
Colutea	■	■	■									
Convolvulus cneorum	■	■										
Cornus	■											
Cornus mas				■								
Coronilla		■	■									
Corylopsis		■	■									
Corylus												■
Cotinus	■											■
Cotoneaster												
Deciduous	■	■								■	■	■
Evergreen	■	■	■									

Pruning Calendar *(continued)*

	spring			summer			autumn			winter		
Cytisus				■	■							
Daboecia						■	■	■	■			
Danae			■									
Daphne	■	■	■									
Desfontainea spinosa	■	■	■									
Deutzia					■	■						
Dipelta						■	■					
Elaeagnus				■	■	■						
Enkianthus				■								
Erica	■	■	■							■	■	■
Escallonia		■				■	■					
Euonymus												
Deciduous	■											■
Evergreen		■	■									
Exochorda					■	■						
x Fatshedera lizei		■	■									
Fatsia japonica			■									
Forsythia		■	■									
Fothergilla			■	■								
Fuchsia	■	■										
Gaultheria				■								
Genista				■	■							
Griselinia		■	■									
x Halimiocistus, Halimium				■	■							
Hamamelis		■	■									
Hebe		■	■									
Helianthemum					■	■						
Helichrysum italicum	■	■										
Hibiscus			■									
Hippophae rhamnoides				■	■							
Hydrangea	■	■										
Hypericum	■	■										
Ilex						■						
Indigofera		■										
Jasminum humile, J. parkeri					■	■						
Kalmia		■			■	■						
Kerria			■	■								
Kolkwitzia					■							
Lavandula		■				■	■					
Lavatera		■	■									
Leonotis leonurus		■	■									
Leptospermum		■	■									
Lespedeza		■	■									
Leucothoe			■									
Leycesteria	■	■	■									
Ligustrum		■	■									
Lonicera												
Evergreen			■	■	■	■						
Winter-flowering		■	■									
Summer-flowering				■	■	■						
Lupinus arboreus		■	■									
Magnolia					■							
Mahonia	■	■	■									
Melianthus major		■	■									
Olearia		■	■									

	spring			summer			autumn			winter		
Osmanthus	■	■	■									
Ozothamnus	■	■	■									
Pachysandra	■	■										
Paeonia				■	■							
Penstemon		■				■						
Perovskia		■										
Philadelphus					■	■						
Phlomis			■	■								
Photinia												
Deciduous										■	■	■
Evergreen		■	■									
Phygelius		■										
Physocarpus opulifolius					■	■						
Pieris			■	■								
Piptanthus	■	■			■							
Pittosporum		■	■									
Potentilla	■	■										
Prunus			■	■								
Pyracantha	■	■										
Rhododendron			■	■	■							
Rhus	■											
Ribes		■	■									
Romneya	■	■										
Rosmarinus officinalis			■									
Rubus				■	■							
Ruta graveolens	■					■						
Salix		■	■									
Salvia		■	■									
Sambucus										■	■	■
Santolina					■	■						
Sarcococca	■	■										
Skimmia			■	■								
Sorbaria										■	■	■
Spartium	■	■										
Spiraea												
Spring-flowering		■	■	■								
Summer-flowering	■											■
Stachyurus		■	■									
Stephanandra						■	■					
Symphoricarpos	■	■	■									
Syringa				■	■							
Tamarix												
Spring-flowering					■	■						
Summer-flowering	■	■										
Thymus					■	■						
Ulex			■	■								
Viburnum												
Winter-flowering	■	■										
V. tinus			■	■								
Spring-flowering				■	■	■						
Vinca	■	■	■									
Weigela					■	■						

Each season divided into three – to represent the three months that make up that season

■ = pruning time

CHAPTER 5

Climbers and Wall Shrubs

Climbers and wall shrubs are extremely versatile plants, even more so in small gardens where space is usually at a premium. Making the best use of horizontal space allows you to clothe your garden to the maximum.

Most gardens have walls and fences that look bare and ugly without something to cover them. Pergolas, gazebos, pillars, tripods, wigwams and rose arches add extra height and interest to the garden, but need some plants scrambling up and over them to ensure they're made the most of. Large trees and shrubs often benefit from having something to clamber up them to extend the seasons of interest.

That's where climbers and wall shrubs come to the fore – and there are lots to choose from, for every garden and every situation.

Some shrubs that are otherwise free-standing can also be used as wall shrubs. These include *Ceanothus*, *Chaenomeles*, *Cotoneaster* (especially *C. horizontalis*), *Cytisus battandieri*, *Forsythia* (especially *F. suspensa*), *Fremontodendron*, *Magnolia grandiflora*, *Phygelius* and *Pyracantha*.

Growing tender climbers and wall shrubs that like plenty of sun on a south-facing wall is an excellent way of helping to ensure their survival, as the protection and heating-absorbing properties of the wall provide extra assistance against cold weather.

When planting at the base of walls, remember that the soil here is usually very dry, so make sure plants are well watered after planting and for the next three months or so, and whenever dry conditions prevail. Mulching the soil with bark or

OPPOSITE: Clematis montana. (Photo: Geoff Hodge)

similar organic material will help maintain soil moisture levels, as will adding a moisture-retention gel (such as those used in summer hanging baskets) to the soil at planting time. The dry conditions can also make some plants more prone to disease – such as mildew on roses and clematis.

INITIAL TRAINING

To ensure that climbers and wall shrubs cover the structure or support evenly, and look attractive and perform to their best ability, some initial training and regular pruning is usually needed. This isn't always so important with rampant climbers that are being left to their own devices, or with those that can take or need annual hard pruning to keep them in their place and ensure regular flowering. But it is important with climbers and wall shrubs that produce a woody framework, such as *Campsis* and *Wisteria* for instance, whose side-shoots are pruned annually to encourage flower formation. However, even rampant climbers benefit from some training and pruning to ensure they don't just become an unattractive mass of tangled stems that flower poorly.

Some climbers (such as ivy) climb using aerial roots that stick to their support, while others use pads or tendrils (such as *Parthenocissus*) in a similar way. Other climbers use twining stems (honeysuckles), twining leaf stalks (*Clematis*), tendrils (*Vitis*) or thorns (roses). The first two will become self-supporting once established, whereas all the other types will probably need regular tying into their support. And all of them need initial tying in until established.

In prominent positions in the garden, you'll always achieve a more pleasing effect if the plants are regularly trained, tied in and pruned when needed. If you leave them to get on with it they'll soon look unruly, messy and very unappealing. Start by tying in growth to cover the support evenly, and prune back strong growth to keep it within bounds and to encourage sideshoots that will help fill in any gaps in the coverage.

By training branches horizontally or in a fan shape, rather than allowing them to grow straight up, you can encourage better flower displays, as this training restricts the flow of sap in the plant and consequently helps initiate flower buds. On walls, fences and trellis this is easy to achieve, whereas climbers growing up narrow supports, such as posts, pillars or wigwams, are best twined around the support in a spiral fashion, rather than being left to grow straight up.

MAINTENANCE PRUNING

To get the most out of your climbers and wall shrubs, remember the principles of 'Why Prune?' detailed in Chapter 1 on page 5. As always, this should be your first reason for getting out the secateurs. Then prune, if necessary, following the information in the A–Z section that follows.

Also remember the pruning techniques described in Chapter 2 on page 15, making the correct types of cut, deadheading where necessary or possible, and finally curing the post-pruning depression.

PRUNING TECHNIQUES

Sadly, many vigorous climbers are left to get on with it for several years until they become a horribly tangled mess of stems; they are then often brutally hacked back to get them under control, which usually results in the plants not flowering for a few years. Even fairly mild, regular pruning – or a 'short back and sides' to 'tidy up' an unruly climber – carried out too often and at the wrong time of year will result in little or no flowers, as this often removes the dormant flower buds. So make sure you follow the directions and pruning time for each plant in the A–Z directory below.

It's particularly important to keep a regular eye on rampant climbers growing on house or garage walls as they can quickly grow into gutters, eaves and even roof spaces if you're not careful, where they can cause unnecessary damage.

In some cases plants can be cut back hard to a framework, but always be guided by the directions given for each individual plant in the A–Z section.

As hard pruning may delay flowering, you can ensure earlier flowering in the year, and even extend the flowering period, by lightly trimming some shoots and cutting back the rest hard. And always follow this up by training in new growth as it develops.

If the main stems are old, bare and unproductive, you may be able to remove them completely to replace them with younger, more productive ones – shoots from ground level or growing low down on the older stems.

CLIMBERS A–Z

Abeliophyllum
White forsythia
Deciduous
This shrub has a lax and open habit, and because it is also slightly frost tender, is best trained against a sunny wall. It produces white flowers in early spring on the previous year's growth.

Select strong stems to form a permanent, informal framework, and tie these to the supports. In subsequent years cut back one in two, or one in three, of the flowered stems annually after flowering. Prune back to low replacement buds or sideshoots near to the base. This will encourage vigorous, free-flowering shoots that help to keep the plant neat and compact.

As plants age, remove completely any old branches that flower poorly, and train in new replacements.

Abutilon
Evergreen and deciduous
Abutilons are half-hardy shrubs, so are often trained against a south-facing wall or are grown

Abutilon megapotamicum. (Photo: Tim Sandall)

indoors. They flower over a long period from spring to autumn on the current season's growth, but can be short-lived.

In early to mid-spring start by removing any shoots that have been damaged by winter weather, any spindly, weak shoots and overcrowded shoots.

A. megapotamicum and hybrids such as 'Kentish Belle' should also have old stems removed once a framework is established, and strong, young shoots tied in to replace them and fill in any gaps.

Actinidia kolomikta
Deciduous
A. kolomikta is a vigorous climber grown for its attractive leaves, which are coloured pink and white.

Prune in late winter or early spring before new growth starts. First, remove any crossing, diseased or over-crowded stems. Over-vigorous and mis-placed shoots can also be pruned in summer.

Cut back young plants to buds 30–40cm (12–16in) above ground level to encourage bushy growth. In the following year, cut back strong sideshoots by two-thirds, and weaker shoots to one or two buds. Once established, and to keep within bounds, shorten the stems by one-third to half.

Occasionally remove an old main stem at its base to encourage new growth.

Neglected plants also can be rejuvenated by cutting back the mass of tangled growth, then pruning back the stems to a healthy bud near to the main framework of branches.

Akebia quinata
Chocolate vine
Deciduous or semi-evergreen
This vigorous climber is grown for its divided foliage and maroon to chocolate-purple flowers in spring.

It doesn't need routine pruning other than the removal of dead or damaged stems in late spring. Once established, *Akebia* can be kept within bounds by pruning once every few years during late spring after flowering. Prune the previous year's growth back by half to two-thirds. Neglected plants can be rejuvenated by cutting back the mass of tangled growth, then pruning the stems back to a healthy bud near to the main framework of branches.

Ampelopsis
Deciduous
This rampant climber is mainly grown for its attractive foliage that turns fiery red in autumn. Being vigorous it needs plenty of space and strong supports, or can be grown through large trees.

It will need to be cut back to keep it within bounds in most gardens, and if grown against walls, to make sure it doesn't block gutters or get under roof tiles. Pruning should be carried out in winter. Where space is restricted, train as many shoots as are needed, remove the rest, and each year cut back all young shoots to within two or three buds of these main stems.

Aristolochia
Dutchman's pipe
Deciduous
This vigorous climber gets its common name from the shape of its yellowish-brown flowers produced in summer.

No routine pruning is required, other than the removal of crossing, weak or damaged stems in late winter or early spring. Further pruning can be carried out after flowering.

To restrict the size of established plants, cut back new growth to within a few buds of the main framework. *Aristolochia* also responds well to more drastic pruning; neglected specimens can be cut back hard in winter by pruning the main framework to a younger sideshoot lower down each main stem.

Berberidopsis
Coral plant
Evergreen

The coral plant is grown for its glossy green leaves and drooping clusters of red, globular flowers in summer and early autumn.

After planting, remove any dead or damaged stems. Once established, little or no pruning is required, other than the removal of weak stems and the thinning out of congested plants in spring after the danger of severe frosts. Old or overgrown plants do not respond well to hard pruning.

Billardiera
Evergreen

This plant is best grown in frost-free conditions. *B. longiflora* produces bell-shaped, greenish-yellow flowers in summer, followed by large, purple-blue fruits.

No routine pruning is required other than the removal of weak, crossing or damaged stems. Overgrown plants can be thinned by cutting back unwanted shoots to within two to three buds of the main framework. Pruning can be carried out in early to mid-spring or late summer (after fruiting).

Bougainvillea
Deciduous or evergreen

Bougainvilleas need frost-free conditions and are best grown under glass. Their insignificant flowers are surrounded by large, colourful bracts that are available in a wide range of colours. They flower on the current season's growth in spring and summer.

To get the best displays, you need to train a framework of well-spaced branches, preferably as a fan. To start, prune back stems hard to stimulate new growth from the base, and tie in the shoots as they develop. Only tie in strong shoots, as

overcrowding can be a problem if too many shoots are selected.

In subsequent years, during late winter or early spring and before new growth starts, cut back the previous year's growth by about two-thirds to three-quarters. Remove any weak or misplaced stems completely. Once it has covered its support, cut back all new growth to just two or three buds from the established framework.

Old plants can be invigorated by removing two or three of the oldest framework stems, cutting back to a younger sideshoot near the base. All other sideshoots on the main framework should be pruned back to two or three buds.

Campsis radicans. (Photo: Tim Sandall)

Campsis
Trumpet vine
Deciduous

Although hardy, trumpet vines need a warm, sunny position to flower well. The large flowers are produced on the current year's growth from late summer to autumn.

It is important to establish a framework of branches. Start by pruning back all stems to 15cm (6in) from the ground to promote strong growth. Select two or three of the strongest shoots, and tie them into the framework; remove the rest.

Once established, prune annually in late winter or early to mid-spring before new growth starts. Cut back the previous season's growth to just two or three buds from the established framework. Remove any weak or misplaced stems completely.

Old plants can be invigorated by removing a couple of the oldest framework stems, cutting them back to a younger sideshoot near the base. Campsis responds well to severe pruning, so neglected plants can be restored by cutting the whole framework back to within 30cm (12in) of the ground.

Ceanothus 'Concha'. *(Photo: Tim Sandall)*

Ceanothus
California lilac
Evergreen and deciduous
Ceanothus are grown for their clusters of mainly blue, but sometimes pink flowers and generally evergreen foliage, although some are deciduous.

Often grown as a free-standing shrub, *Ceanothus* – especially evergreen ones – are often better trained as a wall shrub to protect them from cold weather. They are covered in dense clusters of mainly blue flowers from mid-spring to early autumn, depending on the cultivar.

Time of pruning depends on flowering time: prune those that flower in spring and early summer after flowering in midsummer; prune those that flower in summer and autumn in spring.

Annual pruning consists of cutting back the previous season's growth by one-third to half, and cutting back or removing shoots growing away from the support.

Neglected evergreens are difficult to renovate as new growth does not easily break from old wood.

Celastrus
Bittersweet
Deciduous
Celastrus is a strong climber grown mainly for its autumn display of fruits. It needs a lot of space and is usually best left to its own devices.

Established plants need little or no routine pruning other than the removal of crossing or damaged stems, or those arching away from the support. Severe pruning will stimulate vigorous leafy growth at the expense of flowers and fruit. New shoots and sideshoots that have grown beyond the support can be cut back to two or three buds from their base. Neglected plants can be cut back hard to within 30cm (12in) of the ground, but flowering will be reduced for a few years. All pruning can be carried out in winter or early spring.

Chaenomeles
Flowering or Japanese quince, japonica
Deciduous
This hardy shrub provides a colourful floral display in spring followed by large quince-like fruit in autumn.

Although *Chaenomeles* is usually grown as a free-standing shrub, it flowers better if trained as a wall shrub and is spur-pruned. All pruning should be carried out in late spring/early summer after flowering.

Start by selecting five or six main branches and tying them into the support as a fan. Once the framework is established, cut back excess growth and help produce the flowering spurs by cutting back all sideshoots to two or three leaves. Late-produced stems can be pruned to two to three buds in winter.

These spur systems may become congested in time and may need thinning out. Plants can be renovated by hard pruning, although drastic pruning is best done over a two- to three-year period.

For pruning as a shrub, see page 35; for pruning as a hedge, *see* page 109.

Clematis
Deciduous and evergreen
Probably no other climber has acquired such a reputation for being difficult to prune – and yet it

is fairly straightforward. If left unpruned, clematis develop into a tangled mass of stems, producing their flowers high up on woody, leafless stems. The aim in pruning is to produce a plant that covers its allotted space, and produces plenty of leafy stems and flowers that can be appreciated without the aid of a stepladder!

The time and amount of pruning depends on when the plant flowers: all clematis are therefore divided into three groups to make the decision easier.

Group 1: winter- and spring-flowering clematis
Group 1 mainly consists of vigorous species that flower in winter or spring on growth formed the previous year, such as *C. alpina*, *C. cirrhosa*, *C. macropetela* and *C. montana*. Little or no pruning is really needed by this group unless the plant is smothering its support or is growing where it's not needed. If you want to restrict their spread, prune back overgrown flowered stems after flowering during late spring/early summer to within 5–8cm (2–3in) of the main framework.

Very overgrown plants can be cut back hard to within 60cm (2ft) of the ground in an attempt to regain control. Although often successful, if there are few or no dormant buds on the remaining stem, then the plant won't reshoot. If successful, the plant should get back into flowering mode in two years.

Group 2
This group contains the hybrids that produce their flowers during late spring and early summer on wood produced the previous year. They also tend to produce flowers in late summer and autumn on the current year's growth. This growth habit can make it difficult to decide on a pruning regime. Luckily, it isn't essential to prune this group either, unless they have become tall and straggly and flowering has reduced. If you do want to prune them, this can be carried out annually or every other year, by cutting back the stems by one-third to half above a strong pair of buds in late winter or early spring.

Group 3
This contains the clematis that flower from July onwards, on growth produced during the current year. This group includes *C. orientalis*, *C. tangutica*, the *C. viticella* and *C. texensis* cultivars, together with numerous large-flowered hybrids. All require hard pruning annually to keep them under control and flowering well. Cut back all the stems to just above the base of the previous year's growth, about 30cm (12in) above soil level in late winter or early spring. Prune to the lowest pair of healthy buds that you can see.

Pruning when planting
If simply left to get on with it, clematis tend to produce a single stem and grow quickly upwards. So at planting, cut back the main stem or stems to the lowest pair of strong buds or leaflets to encourage bushier growth. Depending on type and timing you may miss some flowers in the first year, but it's well worth it.

Make sure that all resulting regrowth is trained to cover the support – preferably in a fan or spiral pattern.

Clianthus
Lobster claw, glory pea
Evergreen or semi-evergreen
This frost-tender sprawling shrub can be grown outside on a sunny, south-facing wall in mild areas. The distinctive salmon-red flowers are produced from spring to midsummer on the previous year's growth.

Although no routine pruning is necessary, pruning when young, and training will improve the display. Pinch out the shoot tips after planting to produce bushy growth from the base, then tie in new growth to the support. Once the support is covered, prune flowering shoots after flowering to restrict the plant's size; at the same time remove any dead or damaged stems. Do not prune too heavily, reducing stems by no more than one-third to just above a well placed sideshoot.

Cotoneaster horizontalis
Herring-bone cotoneaster
Deciduous
C. horizontalis makes an excellent wall shrub, especially for a north-facing aspect. It is covered in white flowers in summer, red berries in autumn, and produces fiery autumnal foliage.

After planting, provide initial support for the main branches. The stems will then grow flat against the wall, but remove any that do grow away from the support.

Remove other unwanted branches in late winter, or as and when you have to, because *C. horizontalis* does not respond well to being cut back hard.

For pruning shrubs, *see* page 38.

Cytisus battandieri. (Photo: Tim Sandall)

Cytisus battandieri
Pineapple broom
Semi-evergreen
The pineapple broom is frost hardy, but prefers the shelter of a sunny, south-facing wall. It flowers from early to midsummer on the current year's growth.

Little or no pruning is required, other than the removal of dead or damaged stems. Wayward stems can be cut back to the main framework, and older plants can be rejuvenated by cutting out one of the older stems to a younger sideshoot low down that can be trained to replace it. Pruning should be carried out after flowering.

Eccremocarpus scaber
Chilean glory flower
Evergreen
This frost-sensitive climber may be cut down to ground level by hard frosts, but usually re-shoots from the base, especially if protected with a mulch. It produces attractive foliage and scarlet to orange trumpet flowers on new growth.

After planting, pinch back all stems to 15cm (6in) to encourage new shoots from the base. In subsequent years, cut back all frost-damaged growth and reduce other stems to 30–60cm (12–24in) from the base in spring. As new growth emerges, cut back the shoots to a strong, healthy bud to encourage bushy growth.

Fallopia baldschuanica (Polygonum baldschuanicum)
Russian vine, mile-a-minute
Deciduous
As its common name suggests, *Fallopia* is a vigorous climber – often invasive, so not suitable for small spaces. It produces white or pale pink flowers all summer.

Fallopia needs no formative pruning, simply space out the stems on the support to provide even coverage. Established plants tend to form an entangled mass of stems, making careful pruning difficult. Simply cut back all stems by around one-third of their length in late winter or early spring; further excess growth can be pruned at any time of year, except during frosty weather.

To renovate overgrown plants, cut back to within 30cm (1ft) of ground level.

Forsythia suspensa
Deciduous
This shrub has a lax, open habit and so is better trained as a wall shrub.

Select strong branches to form the framework of the plant and tie these into the supports. After flowering, cut back the flowered shoots to one or two buds of the main framework branches. In time, you may need to train in young stems to the framework to replace older branches.

Neglected plants can be renovated by hard pruning in winter or spring; this is best carried out over two years.

Fremontodendron
Evergreen
This shrub produces large, spectacular yellow flowers from summer to autumn on the current year's growth. It is not completely hardy, so is best grown as a wall shrub on a south-facing aspect.

Once the main framework has been established,

little or no pruning is usually required, other than the removal of dead or damaged stems. Wayward stems and outward-growing shoots need to be shortened, cutting back to sideshoots that grow parallel to the wall after the first flush of flowers in summer.

Old and neglected plants do not respond to severe pruning and are best replaced.

When pruning fremontodendron, be careful of the irritant hairs that cover the leaves and stems. These can cause severe itching, especially if the sap gets into the eyes, so it is a good idea to wear goggles and gloves whenever handling this plant.

Garrya elliptica 'James Roof'. *(Photo: Tim Sandall)*

Garrya elliptica
Silk-tassel bush
Evergreen
Garrya is a shrub grown for its handsome, leathery leaves and attractive catkins in winter and spring.

After planting, prune to retain two or three main framework stems, and cut back all sideshoots that are growing away from the wall. Once established, and the framework or support is covered, cut back any badly placed shoots in early to mid-spring as the catkins fade, but before new growth begins.

Renovate overgrown plants over a three- or four-year period, as regrowth is vigorous, by cutting back to the main framework branches.

Hedera
Ivy
Evergreen
Ivies are grown for their attractive leaves, available in a range of single and variegated colours, shapes

and sizes. They are very vigorous and can soon spread out of control.

Prune during early spring before new growth starts to keep plants within bounds, and to keep them tidy. Cut back wayward shoots to just above a bud. Remove overcrowded shoots entirely, as well as those growing away from the support. This can also be done throughout the summer and early autumn.

Ivies respond well to severe pruning, so old, neglected plants can be reinvigorated by hard pruning – cutting back to within 30cm (12in) of the base.

Hibbertia
Button flower, guinea gold vine
Evergreen
This tender climber needs frost-free conditions and produces saucer-shaped, bright yellow flowers in summer.

After planting, pinch out the growing tips of each stem to encourage sideshoots and bushy growth. Tie in stems until they twine naturally. Little or no pruning is required, other than the removal of dead, damaged and congested stems in early spring. *Hibbertia* does not respond to hard pruning.

Humulus
Hop
Deciduous
The hop plant is a herbaceous climber grown for its foliage and attractive hops. It will die down to ground level each year, but produces lots of regrowth in spring.

Young plants do not need any formative pruning and established plants can be left to get on with it. In early to mid-spring, simply cut back all of last year's shoots to ground level, and tie in new shoots around the base of the support.

Hydrangea
Climbing hydrangea
Deciduous and evergreen
Climbing hydrangeas are popular, vigorous wall shrubs that are useful for shaded walls; they produce glossy foliage and heads of creamy white summer flowers. They can take a few years to become established, but they are then quite vigorous.

Hydrangea anomala subsp. *petiolaris.*
(Photo: Tim Sandall)

Jasminum nudiflorum. (Photo: Tim Sandall)

No formative pruning is needed, just tie in young shoots to their supports until they become self-supporting. Little or no routine pruning is required, and pruning is best kept to a minimum, apart from removing the flowered shoots after flowering. At the same time, reduce overlong shoots and outward growing sideshoots by cutting back to a healthy bud.

To rejuvenate old and neglected plants, hard prune in winter/early spring to leave only the main framework branches. Such hard pruning will reduce flowering, so is often best spread over three to four years.

For pruning hydrangea shrubs, *see* page 43.

Jasminum nudiflorum
Winter jasmine
Deciduous
Winter jasmine is a valuable wall shrub producing masses of yellow flowers during winter, formed on the previous year's shoots.

Start by creating a framework of well spaced branches over the support; it may pay to cut back the plant by up to two-thirds to produce strong basal growth.

Once established, annual pruning is needed immediately after flowering, otherwise the new growth covers old growth causing lots of untidy-looking dead wood. Cut back shoots that are not needed in order to extend the framework to two or three buds of their base. To keep plants within bounds you can also remove unwanted and wayward shoots.

Winter jasmine also tolerates hard pruning, so neglected and overgrown plants can be reinvigorated by cutting back to within around 60cm (2ft) of the base.

Jasminum officinale
Common jasmine, summer jasmine
Deciduous
This white-flowered, scented climber produces flowers on sideshoots from the previous year's growth, and terminally on new growth throughout summer and autumn.

Start by creating a framework of well spaced branches over the support; it may pay to cut back the plant by up to two-thirds to produce strong basal growth.

Once established, cut out overcrowded growth and weak shoots, and prune flowered shoots to a sideshoot or bud near their base after flowering has finished.

Common jasmine tolerates hard pruning, so neglected plants can be invigorated by cutting back to 60cm (2ft) of the base. New growth will be vigorous, but may not flower for a couple of years.

Other jasmines treated in the same way include *J. beesianum*, *J. polyanthum* and *J.* × *stephanense*.

For pruning *Jasminum humile* and *J. parkeri, see* page 44.

Lapageria
Chilean bell flower
Evergreen
Lapageria is grown for its leathery leaves and spectacular waxy, bell-shaped flowers. It needs some protection from cold winds and frosts.

It requires minimum pruning – simply remove dead or damaged shoots in early spring. It won't tolerate hard pruning, so make sure plants are tidied up annually and trained carefully on to the support.

Lathyrus latifolius
Perennial pea
Deciduous
The hardy perennial pea is perfect for training up supports or scrambling through other plants and flowers all summer.

After planting, pinch out the growing tips to encourage bushy growth. During the summer, tidy up plants by removing weak, damaged or dead growth. Remove faded flower heads to prevent seed production and to ensure continuous flowering. In spring, cut back all dead growth to ground level before new growth starts.

Lonicera
Honeysuckle
Deciduous, evergreen and semi-evergreen
Honeysuckles are invaluable summer- and often autumn-flowering climbers. Some species also produce autumn berries.

The common honeysuckle, *L. periclymenum*, flowers from early to late summer at the tips of short sideshoots produced the previous year; it should therefore be pruned after flowering. After planting, cut back stems by up to two-thirds to encourage bushy growth. Tie in the shoots to form the main framework. Once established, prune flowered shoots by up to one-third, and remove weak and crowded growth. If growing plants up pillars, posts or similar supports, the sideshoots can be cut back to two to three buds from the main

stem. Once it has reached the top of its support, tip back the shoots to encourage flowering side-shoots to develop.

To rejuvenate old plants, cut back all stems to within 30–60cm (1–2ft) of the base in late winter or early spring; thin out the resulting shoots as necessary. Plants treated this way will take a couple of years to start flowering again.

Other species treated in the same way include *L.* × *americana*, *L.* × *brownii*, *L. caprifolium*, *L.* × *heckrottii*, *L. sempervirens*, *L.* × *tellmanniana* and *L. tragophylla*.

The Japanese honeysuckle, *L. japonica*, flowers in summer and autumn on the current year's growth, and is pruned in early spring. Initial training is the same as for *L. periclymenum*. Then tip back shoots once they reach the required height to encourage flowering sideshoots to develop. Established plants can become over-congested if left unpruned, so thin out the main stems every few years by cutting back to a newer sideshoot lower down. Neglected plants can become a mass of stems if not pruned regularly – with flowers just on the top. Give a 'short back and sides', then reduce the number of main stems, removing any awkwardly placed or crossing stems. Plants can be renovated in the same way as *L. periclymenum*. *L. henryi* is treated in the same way.

For pruning shrubby honeysuckles, *see* page 46.

Magnolia grandiflora
Evergreen
This handsome evergreen tree produces creamy white flowers in late summer. In cool climates it is often trained against a sunny, sheltered wall.

After planting, tie the leading shoot vertically to supporting wires, tie in sideshoots at an angle of 45 degrees, and cut out all forward- and backward-facing shoots. In the second year, sideshoots can be untied, lowered and tied in horizontally. Any new sideshoots can also be trained at 45 degrees. In subsequent years, continue to tie in sideshoots – first at an angle, and then the following year horizontally. Tie in shoots to fill in the framework, and in the summer remove unwanted shoots. Once the allotted space has been filled, take out the shoot tips in summer.

To renovate a neglected plant, cut back all

branches to a main framework over two to three years. Then select and train new shoots as above.

Parthenocissus

Boston ivy, Virginia creeper
Deciduous

Parthenocissus are grown for their large, handsome foliage and its fiery autumn colours. They are vigorous climbers suitable for large walls or lengths of fencing.

Plants need no formative pruning, but new shoots should be tied to their supports for the first couple of years. Once established, plants need an annual tidy-up in autumn after the foliage has fallen, or in early winter to keep them within bounds and to remove unwanted shoots. *Parthenocissus* can also be lightly trimmed in summer if necessary.

Old and neglected plants respond well to severe pruning and can be cut back to within 90cm (3ft) of the base in winter.

Parthenocissus tricuspidata. (Photo: Tim Sandall)

Passiflora

Passion flower
Evergreen or semi-evergreen

Passion flowers are grown for their attractive foliage, unique summer flowers and sometimes their edible fruit.

The best way to grow passion flowers is to establish a framework of stems spaced about 15–20cm (6–8in) apart on a sturdy support. To fan-train, nip out the growing points after planting to encourage

Passiflora caerulea 'Constance Elliott'.
(Photo: Geoff Hodge)

shoots from the base and tie in up to five of the strongest shoots to form the fan shape. If training along wires, select a single stem to grow vertically and pinch back sideshoots until it has reached the top of the support. Sideshoots can then be trained horizontally to form the framework.

Once the plant is established, prune it every spring to remove dead, damaged and overcrowded stems, and shorten any others to keep the plant within bounds. Then cut back new growth to within 15cm (6in) of the established framework. After flowering, cut back the flowered shoots to within two to three leaves of the framework branches.

Neglected plants can be reinvigorated to some extent in spring by cutting back one-third of the oldest stems to a new sideshoot near the base.

Replace old specimens with new plants rather than attempt drastic pruning.

Plumbago

Cape leadwort
Evergreen or semi-evergreen

Plumbago is grown for its beautiful powder-blue summer flowers produced throughout summer and often into winter on the current year's growth. It is not frost hardy, but can be grown outside in mild areas on a south-facing wall.

On planting, pinch out the growing points to encourage shoots from the base, and tie in up to five of the strongest shoots to form the framework. Tie in the shoots to supports as they grow, and then nip out the growing point once they have reached the required height, to encourage sideshoots.

Once established, prune annually in late winter or early to mid-spring to maintain the main framework. Remove completely all weak, damaged, overcrowded and badly placed shoots. Then prune back all sideshoots to two or three buds from their base. As flowers fade, the plant can be deadheaded to encourage further flowering

To renovate an old plant, cut back all the shoots to within 30cm (12in) of the base; if new growth is not forthcoming or is weak, then the plant should be replaced.

Pyracantha

Firethorn
Evergreen
Pyracanthas make fine wall-trained shrubs, being particularly useful for shady and north-facing aspects, especially when trained as a fan. They are covered with white flowers in summer and colourful berries in autumn and winter.

Although pyracantha is usually pruned in mid-spring, wall-trained plants can be pruned for a second time from mid- to late summer, shortening the new growth to expose the developing berries and so making the most of the display.

Start by selecting five or six main branches, and then tie them into the support to produce the permanent framework. Train these out in a fan shape. Remove outward-growing shoots, those not needed for the framework, and any shoots growing beyond the support in spring.

For pruning as a shrub, *see* page 52; for pruning as a hedge, *see* page 109.

Rhodochiton

Evergreen
This is a half-hardy perennial climber, often grown annually from seed as it is not frost hardy, but can be grown indoors. It produces unusual maroon-purple tubular flowers set off by an expanded bell.

On planting, pinch out the growing tips to encourage bushy growth.

Established plants are pruned in early to mid-spring to remove dead or damaged shoots and those that are growing beyond the support. This plant doesn't tolerate hard pruning.

Ribes speciosum

Fuchsia-flowered currant
Deciduous
Although *R. speciosum* is hardy, it flowers better if grown against a warm wall; in this situation it will be covered in drooping red flowers in mid- to late spring.

Shoots can be trained in as needed, but the effect is much more pleasing if they are trained as a fan. Once established, plants need little pruning, except to remove an old framework branch in late spring/early summer after flowering, if flowering is reduced, and to train in young growth.

An old, neglected plant can be renovated by pruning all the main stems back to 30cm (12in) from the ground.

For pruning shrubby *Ribes, see* page 53.

Schizophragma

Deciduous
Looking similar to climbing hydrangea, *Schizophragma* produces white lacecap flowers in summer. Like the hydrangea, it is also useful for shady, north-facing walls, but flowers best with some sun.

Little or no regular pruning is needed, apart from removing the flowered shoots as they fade. If necessary, long, vigorous shoots can be cut back to a sideshoot lower down. Cut back overly long shoots by about two-thirds to keep the plant within bounds after flowering.

Neglected plants do not respond well to severe pruning, so cut back over several years by pruning back one older shoot to a new sideshoot near to the base.

Solanum

Potato vine
Semi-evergreen
Potato vines are grown for their star-shaped flowers, produced on the current year's growth. They will tolerate light frost and can be grown as free-standing shrubs, but are better against a warm wall.

After planting, remove the growing tips to promote bushy growth. Select four or five shoots to form the main framework and tie them to the support; keep tying in as they grow.

Solanum crispum 'Glasnevin'. *(Photo: Tim Sandall)*

Established plants should be pruned annually during spring (after any cold or frosty weather) to thin out overcrowded growth and restrict its size. Cut back shoots not needed to extend the framework to two or three buds of their base.

Neglected plants do not respond to severe pruning. Instead, cut out one in three stems from the framework, starting with the oldest, every year. Ideally, cut back to a newer sideshoot lower down.

Trachelospermum
Star jasmine, Confederate jasmine
Evergreen
The star jasmine is grown for its sweetly scented, jasmine-like flowers produced in summer and early autumn on old wood, and its glossy, leathery leaves. It is a vigorous scrambler when established, tending to produce a mass of entangled shoots if not pruned regularly.

It needs no formative pruning: just tie in young growth to the support. In early spring, remove weak shoots and thin out overcrowded, congested growth. Any outward-growing shoots can be trained back to the support or removed, and overlong shoots can be tipped back to just above a flowering spur.

To renovate old plants, cut back all growth by up to two-thirds.

Vitis
Ornamental vine
Deciduous
Ornamental vines are mainly grown for their attractive foliage, although some do produce small edible/inedible bunches of grapes.

It is important to carry out any major pruning during winter before the sap begins to rise, otherwise the plant may bleed to death.

After planting, pinch out the growing tips and select two or three shoots to form the main framework. Once the framework is established, shorten all the previous year's growth to two or three buds of the main branches. Excessive growth can be pruned back to a bud in summer.

Old plants respond well to severe pruning, and can be cut back to buds about 90cm (3ft) from the ground during winter.

For pruning fruiting vines, *see* page 135.

Wisteria
Deciduous
Wisteria is extremely versatile and can be trained against walls, grown through pergolas where its blooms can be seen cascading overhead, or it can be trained to form a standard. Whichever way you grow them, you will need to prune them properly if you want a spectacular display of flowers.

Start by training the stems to cover the framework or support. Then you can prune for flowers, which needs to be done twice a year – in summer, about two months after flowering, and again in winter.

By midsummer it will have produced masses of long, whippy stems, which if not required to cover the support, should be pruned back to within five or seven leaves from the main stem. In winter cut back the stems that were pruned in summer to within two or three buds of their base. If you did not prune in summer you can cut back the whippy stems.

This pruning system builds up a mass of small stubs or spurs that will flower profusely the following year.

Pruning Calendar

	spring			summer			autumn			winter		
Abeliophyllum		■	■									
Abutilon	■	■										
Actinidia kolomikta	■			■	■	■						■
Akebia quinata			■									
Ampelopsis										■	■	■
Aristolochia	■				■	■					■	■
Berberidopsis		■	■									
Billardiera	■	■				■						
Bougainvillea	■											■
Campsis	■	■										■
Ceanothus												
Summer/autumn flowering		■	■									
Spring/early summer flowering					■	■						
Celastrus	■									■	■	■
Chaenomeles			■	■	■							
Clematis (Group 1)			■	■								
Clematis (Group 2 & 3)	■											■
Clianthus						■	■					
Cotoneaster horizontalis												■
Cytisus battandieri						■						
Eccremocarpus scaber	■	■										
Fallopia baldschuanica	■											■
Forsythia suspensa		■	■				(renovation only)			■	■	■
Fremontodendron					■	■						
Garrya elliptica	■	■										
Hedera	■			■	■	■	■					
Hibbertia	■											
Humulus	■	■										
Hydrangea	■			■			■			■	■	■
Jasminum nudiflorum	■	■										
Jasminum officinale				■	■	■	■					
Lapageria	■											

	spring			summer			autumn			winter		
Lathyrus latifolius	■	■		■	■	■						
Lonicera periclymenum					■	■	■					
Lonicera japonica	■											
Magnolia grandiflora				■	■	■						
Parthenocissus				■	■	■			■	■		
	(light trimming only)											
Passiflora	■	■					■		■			
Plumbago	■	■										■
Pyracantha		■			■		■					
Rhodochiton	■	■										■
Ribes speciosum			■	■								
Schizophragma							■		■			
Solanum		■	■									
Trachelospermum	■											
Vitis										■	■	■
Wisteria					■	■				■	■	

Each season divided into three – to represent the three months that make up that season

■ = pruning time

CHAPTER 6

Roses

Maybe not as popular as they once were, roses still have an important part to play in gardens. There's a huge selection to choose from, and a rose for every purpose:

- The bush hybrid teas and floribundas can't be beaten for flower power, producing their colourful blooms for months on end right through the summer and well into the autumn. Hybrid teas bear their blooms on long, strong stems, whereas floribundas produce theirs in clusters with several blooms within each cluster open at any one time.
- Climbers and ramblers are invaluable for clothing walls, fences, arches and pergolas.
- Ground-cover roses do just that, and make use of what could otherwise be bare soil.
- Miniatures and patio varieties can be grown at the front of beds or in small containers on the patio or even in windowboxes.
- Standards and weeping standards provide structural height.
- The diverse group known as shrub roses contain a wealth of different types, from low-growing dwarfs to towering giants, many with excellent flower shapes, fantastic scent, autumn hips and a range of different uses.

Their decline in popularity is certainly due to the fact that they can succumb to diseases, but also because it is thought that pruning is difficult and complicated. But it needn't be that way.

Old books and other references will tell you always to prune just above an outward-facing bud

OPPOSITE: Roses will brighten up a garden for months on end. (Photo: Tim Sandall)

using a slanting cut; yes, that is the traditional way that usually gives the best results, but you don't have to be so exacting. Pruning to an outward-facing bud does help to keep the centre of the plant open and to reduce disease problems, but it can make the plant wider. And slanting cuts aren't essential – pruning just above the bud is the only real thing to remember.

When pruning, always be on the lookout for the four Ds: dead, diseased, dying and damaged stems, plus those that are rubbing, and cross from one side of the plant to the other.

One method of bush and shrub rose 'pruning' that has become quite popular with some is to use a powered hedgetrimmer! This rough and ready method has shown to produce good results, although the number and quality of blooms does start to decline after about four or five years if it is carried out every year. To overcome this and ensure quality blooms in profusion every year, simply replace the hedgetrimmer with the secateurs every three or four years.

DEADHEADING ROSES

Once flowering has finished, those roses that can flower again (repeat flowering) and that don't produce attractive hips in the autumn are best deadheaded. This ensures the plant puts all its energy into producing more flowers, rather than seeds.

The older, prescribed method of deadheading roses was to remove the faded flower plus about 10–15cm (4–6in) of stem below it. This is no longer recommended as the best way of doing it, and the more leaves that are left on the plant, the more energy it can produce to make further flowers. Now it is considered best simply to snap off the faded flower head with your thumb and forefinger.

Rosa 'Summer Lady' = 'Tanydal'. *(Photo: Tim Sandall)*

SUCKERS

Most roses are grafted or budded on to a rootstock, in which case there is always the possibility of suckers being produced. You'll often read that you can distinguish between the rose cultivar and the sucker because the sucker will produce leaves made up of seven leaflets. But this isn't always the case, and the best way of checking is to follow the stem back to where it originates: if it is above the graft union (where the cultivar joins the rootstock) it is from the cultivar, and if it is below it is from the rootstock. As with all suckers, rather than cut it off (which can leave behind dormant buds that can reshoot), carefully tear it off, which will remove the dormant buds.

There are still plenty of people who would prefer to treat their roses individually and prune with loving care. For those people we have provided full details in this chapter.

BUSH ROSES: HYBRID TEAS AND FLORIBUNDAS

Bush roses are the most popular types, mainly because of their very long flowering period, right through summer and into autumn. Hybrid teas may now be referred to as large-flowered roses, and floribundas as cluster-flowered roses, according to their flowering habits.

These benefit from hard pruning in their first year. Those planted when dormant can be pruned immediately after planting, cutting back stems to 10–15cm (4–6in) from ground level. Containerized roses planted in full growth are best simply tidied up to remove dead, weak and spindly growth, and then pruned quite hard the following winter or early spring.

Hybrid Teas

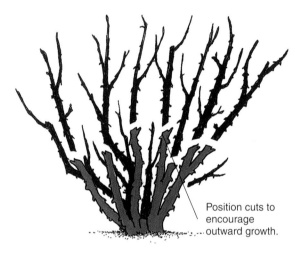

Position cuts to encourage outward growth.

Pruning established hybrid tea roses.

The main pruning is carried out in late winter or early spring, depending on weather conditions, preferably before the growth buds start shooting.

All spindly growth should be removed, as it is unlikely to flower and will be the first to succumb to disease. All remaining healthy stems should be shortened to 15–20cm (6–8in). Generally speaking, the thinner the stem, the harder you prune.

Floribundas

Floribundas are generally more vigorous than hybrid teas, and pruning is similar, but less severe. As with hybrid teas, annual pruning is carried out from late winter to early spring.

Strong shoots of newly planted floribundas should be cut back to 15–23cm (6–9in) from the ground; weak ones should be removed entirely. In subsequent years, as with all pruning, start by cutting out all dead, diseased, rubbing and crossing stems. If the centre of the bush is crowded, prune out some of the old shoots completely to keep the centre open.

Then shorten all the main one-year-old shoots by about one-third to within 23–30cm (9–12in) of the ground. Laterals or sideshoots can be shortened to two or three buds from the main stem. Prune back any older wood to within 15–23cm (6–9in) of the ground.

As with hybrid teas, it is a good idea to tip back the main growth in late autumn or early winter, and to cut out any soft, unripe shoots. In windy, exposed areas, cutting back by up to one-third will help reduce wind rock and subsequent damage to the roots.

MINIATURE ROSES

The pruning of miniatures is similar to that recommended for hybrid teas, although you should avoid cutting back too hard, especially after planting. When pruning, cut out weak and very spindly shoots, and tip back stronger stems to 10–15cm (4–6in) from the ground.

Miniature roses sometimes produce over-vigorous shoots, which can spoil the shape of the plant; these should be cut back or even removed completely in order to maintain the plant's balance and appearance.

Patio and Polyantha Roses

Patio and polyantha roses can also be included here. Patio roses are simply small cultivars of cluster-flowered roses; polyanthas are compact bushes with tight clusters of small flowers.

The pruning of both is the same as for floribundas, just on a smaller scale, but do not cut back newly planted bushes too severely.

These roses often produce a mass of thin, twiggy growth. After this unproductive growth has been removed, the main stems should be reduced by about one-third to a healthy bud or sideshoot. Completely remove any over-long shoots that spoil the shape of the bush.

Pruning a shrub rose. (Photo: Tim Sandall)

SHRUB ROSES

These are the old-fashioned roses, often called Old English, and include all the species roses plus the albas, bourbons, damasks and gallicas among others. They all belong to groups that existed before the introduction of hybrid teas and floribundas.

There is a huge diversity among this group, but most only require light pruning. Many flower just once in summer – although some do repeat flower – and will bloom freely for many years with little or no pruning.

When planting shrub roses in spring, prune out dead, damaged or weak growth, but leave the remaining strong stems unpruned.

Unlike bush roses, shrub roses generally flower on older wood and should be allowed to develop naturally, maintained by light but regular pruning and with a balance of older and young, vigorous growth.

Many shrub roses have an arching habit and need plenty of space as a result, so just shortening the stems simply to restrict their spread will spoil their graceful shape.

Single-Flowering Shrub Roses

Prune in late summer once flowering has finished. The main thing to remember is to keep plants free of dead, diseased and damaged wood, crossing or rubbing branches and thin, spindly growth. Prune the main stems lightly. Avoid an excessive build-up of older, unproductive wood crowding the centre. If the plants become leggy and bare at the base, remove one or two stems, back to near ground level, to encourage new, strong growth.

Rosa 'Gruss an Teplitz'. (Photo: Tim Sandall)

Repeat-Flowering Shrubs

Try to maintain a balanced framework of branches by reducing strong new growth by up to one-third, and shortening strong sideshoots to two or three buds; do this in late winter to early spring. Once the plants are mature, cut back some of the older main stems to their base: this encourages vigorous new shoots that will flower the following summer.

GROUND-COVER ROSES

These roses are extremely useful for covering relatively large areas of ground, for instance a bank. They need very little pruning, apart from removing wayward growth and to keep them under control.

In late winter or early spring, start by removing any dead, diseased or damaged stems. Then tip-prune the remaining stems to encourage bushiness, and finally shorten any sideshoots that extend over their allotted boundary.

NEW ENGLISH ROSES

This is the name given to a recent selection of roses bred by David Austin Roses. They are a cross between old, shrub roses and more modern hybrid tea or floribunda roses. The resulting plants have the advantages of both groups – disease resistance, long flowering period, good scent and flower form.

Their growth habits, and so their pruning method, vary widely and so no overall pruning guide can be given. They should not be pruned as hard as hybrid tea or floribunda roses, but generally benefit from light cutting back when dormant.

CLIMBING AND RAMBLER ROSES

Although these two types of rose are seen as being similar, there are significant differences between them – not only in how they grow and flower but, more importantly, how they are pruned.

Climbers generally produce large flowers in smaller trusses on stiffer stems, and these can be produced in several flushes over a long period. Ramblers have long, pliable stems and bear trusses of smaller flowers just once in the summer.

Climbers are best for trellis, short lengths of fence or wall, and posts and pillars. Ramblers, being more vigorous, are better given plenty of room and can be used as ground cover or trained into trees.

Climbing Roses

Climbing roses need a suitable support, such as a trellis or a series of horizontal wires, to which the shoots can be tied. If using wires, place the lowest 45cm (18in) off the ground and space other wires 30cm (12in) apart. If training plants up pillars, arches or pergolas, twist the main shoots gently around the uprights to encourage flowering shoots to form low down.

To ensure plenty of flowers it is important to train as many main stems as possible horizontally.

Pruning climbing roses

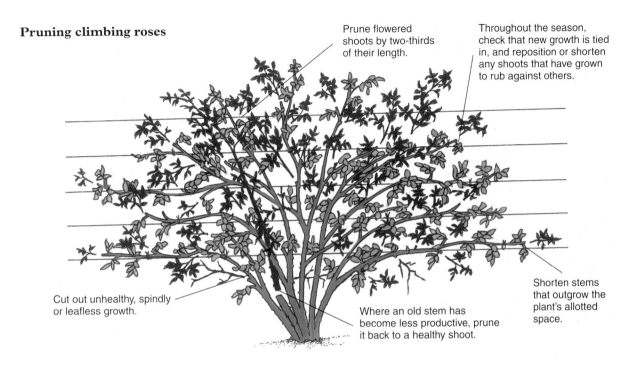

Prune flowered shoots by two-thirds of their length.

Throughout the season, check that new growth is tied in, and reposition or shorten any shoots that have grown to rub against others.

Cut out unhealthy, spindly or leafless growth.

Where an old stem has become less productive, prune it back to a healthy shoot.

Shorten stems that outgrow the plant's allotted space.

If stems are allowed to grow vertically upwards they become bare at the base and flowers are produced high up. The flowers are produced on a framework of mature stems, which should be maintained for as long as possible.

After planting, do not prune any of the main stems, just remove dead, damaged and weak growth. Fan out the main stems, spacing them evenly, and tie in sideshoots to the horizontal wires as they develop to form a well structured framework.

If the main stems are slow to branch, you can tip-prune them to the first strong bud to encourage sideshoots; otherwise leave them to fill the available space.

When the rose is established and has filled the allotted space, excessive growth can be cut back at any time. The main pruning is carried out in late autumn or winter, when flowered sideshoots can be pruned back by two-thirds.

In subsequent years, one or two of the oldest stems could be cut back harder to a lower new shoot, which can be tied in to fill the gap created.

Old and neglected climbers can have unproductive main stems cut back to the base to stimulate new growth.

Rambler Roses

Ramblers should be pruned after planting to encourage new growth from the base. Start by removing dead, damaged or twiggy growth and then cut back the main stems to about 30–50cm (12–20in). Carefully train the remaining and resulting new shoots in a fan shape, and tie them horizontally.

Once the allotted space is covered, you can thin and shorten excess growth after flowering. Ramblers make more new growth from the base than climbing roses, so you can remove one in three of the oldest stems. If space is restricted, all flowered stems can be cut out and new ones tied in their space, and sideshoots shortened by about two-thirds.

Old and overgrown ramblers can be pruned in autumn or winter. Start by removing all dead,

Pruning rambler roses

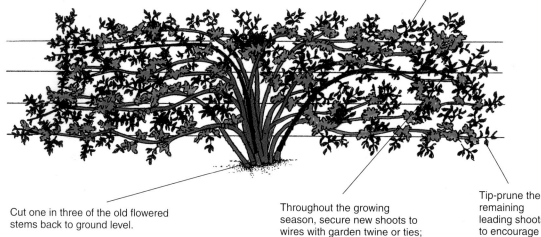

Shorten sideshoots by about two-thirds to encourage them to develop flowering sideshoots the next season.

Cut one in three of the old flowered stems back to ground level.

Throughout the growing season, secure new shoots to wires with garden twine or ties; allow room for them to expand.

Tip-prune the remaining leading shoots to encourage branching.

diseased, dying, damaged and weak growth. Then reduce the framework to a maximum of six young, vigorous stems. Reduce the length of the sideshoots on the remaining stems by two-thirds, and tip-prune the leader to encourage branching. Tie in the resulting new growth in summer while it is still flexible.

Rosa Bonica = 'Meidomonac'. *(Photo: Tim Sandall)*

STANDARD ROSES

A standard rose is where a named rose cultivar is budded on to the top of a rose stem (usually *Rosa rugosa* or *R. laxa*), around 1.2m (4ft) tall, to produce a small rose 'tree' with a flowering head. Half standards and even quarter standards are also available; having shorter stems, these plants are not as high and are suitable for smaller gardens.

The head is pruned in a similar way to a hybrid tea or floribunda (depending on which cultivars are used), although pruning is generally not as hard; stems can be pruned back to seven to ten buds from the graft union.

As well as dealing with any suckers that develop, always keep the main stem free from any side growth by cutting out or, better still, rubbing off any shoots as they appear.

Weeping Standards

Weeping standards are similar, except that a rambler or climbing rose is grafted to the top of the stem, producing stems that hang or weep down, rather than grow up.

These plants are pruned in summer to remove all the flowering shoots. This will leave the younger growth that will flower the following year. Better results are achieved by keeping the centre of the head open by pruning to an outward-facing bud or sideshoot.

Weeping standards are often grown using a wire training frame (similar to an inverted hanging basket) to which the stems are tied; this helps keep the head under control. This way any shoots, especially wayward ones, can be trained to fill in the head and ensure even growth, coverage and flowering.

RENOVATION

Very old roses that don't flower very well and those that haven't been pruned for many years are often worth replacing. However, it's always worth trying to renovate them – even roses that are twenty to thirty years old can be brought back to flowering life.

The best time to carry out renovation work is autumn or winter when the plants are dormant; even ramblers that are normally pruned after flowering are best tackled at this time, although it might mean a year with no flowers. As always, follow up such severe pruning by feeding (using a granular rose fertilizer) and mulching around the stems.

Bush and shrub roses should be cut back to within 2.5–5cm (1–2in) of ground level. Climbing roses can have one in three stems cut back to 30cm (12in) from ground level; repeat with the uncut stems over the following two years. Rambler roses should have old stems removed completely to leave just three or four of the youngest, strongest stems. Then cut back any sideshoots to 7.5–10cm (3–4in).

Renovating a bush rose

Shorten the remaining strong, healthy stems to reduce the height of the bush by at least half.

Where possible, cut back older main stems to strong new shoots arising low down.

Saw away dead stumps at the base of the plant.

Remove completely any very old, unhealthy or spindly stems.

CHAPTER 7

Ornamental Trees

A well grown tree can provide a striking central focal point to any garden. Trees provide structure and leaf canopy, many have coloured foliage, or foliage that turns beautiful colours in the autumn, some produce fruit in autumn and winter, and yet others have coloured and ornamental bark.

Not all trees are massive: many are suitable for even the smallest of gardens. But where a large tree has been chosen (or inherited, in the case of moving into a house with an established garden) and has outgrown its position, the worst thing you can do is to constantly 'butcher' it to keep it within bounds. This often results in unattractive growth patterns and, in some cases, can weaken or even kill the tree.

When choosing a tree, always take into account its final height, and try and restrict yourself to initial formative training and pruning to produce a well shaped, balanced shape where this is necessary. Most trees that are bought from a nursery or garden centre have already had their initial training, but untrained whips and very young trees usually need some formative training if they are to achieve the desired shape and overall effect.

Once established, many trees require little or no further pruning, apart from removing dead, dying, damaged, diseased or unwanted growth, such as branches that are too low, have spread too far, are rubbing against each other, or generally spoil the overall shape or appearance.

Careful, selective renovation pruning can rejuvenate many neglected trees, but this is often best left to a trained arboriculturist or tree surgeon; *see* page 90 for details on how to choose a tree surgeon.

OPPOSITE: Alnus glutinosa. (Photo: Tim Sandall)

And always bear in mind that some trees are protected by tree preservation orders (TPOs), especially in areas of outstanding beauty. Find out more on page 90.

TREE SHAPES AND FORMS

When choosing a tree it is also important to recognize its overall shape and growth pattern. This not only determines how it will look in the garden, but also, in many cases, how it should be trained and pruned.

Central-leader Standard

Most trees are best grown as a central-leader standard, where the main trunk persists throughout their length, terminating in a distinct leading shoot. Some trees (such as red oak) grow naturally like this, while others can be produced by gradually removing lower branches over a number of years to leave a clear trunk. The clear trunk can be anything from 1m (3ft) for small trees to 3m (10ft) for very vigorous, tall tree species, and depends on how clear you want the trunk to be.

Branch-headed Standard

These have a single clear trunk, which then branches to form a head or crown. It happens naturally in horse chestnut, and can be produced by cutting back a young tree's main stem at a given height to stimulate branching, or by top-grafting on to a rootstock, such as in some cherries. Any lower branches on the main stem should be gradually removed.

Shorter half standards are often more suited to less vigorous, lower-growing species.

Feathered Tree

Some species naturally retain their lower branches rather than losing them as they develop into standards; for example silver birch and conifers. The main trunk may be clothed in branches right down to ground level.

Multi-stemmed Tree

These trees, or in some cases large shrubs, have several main stems coming from ground level or on a short stem, or leg, above ground level.

Weeping Tree

Weeping standards either form naturally, such as weeping willow, or are produced by grafting a weeping or prostrate cultivar on to the top of a rootstock stem. Others, such as the weeping birch, naturally form weeping, feathered trees, although the lower branches on the main stem are usually removed to show off the trunk.

Fastigiate Tree

A narrow, columnar tree with upright branches that often completely clothe the main trunk. It is a natural growth habit and, unlike the other forms, cannot be produced by training and pruning.

Pleaching

Pleaching is a specialized growing method that involves weaving together the branches of a row of trees, together with formal pruning to produce a hedge or barrier 'on stilts'. The main species used are *Carpinus*, *Crataegus*, *Fagus*, *Ilex*, *Salix* and *Tilia*, although any tree species that responds well to regular pruning can be used. It is a labour-intensive feature, takes many years to achieve and is only really suitable for the largest of gardens. Even more elaborate are walks or tunnels produced by two lines of trees, the most popular being laburnum tunnels where you can appreciate the hanging flowers.

PRUNING TECHNIQUES FOR TREES

Although the general principles of pruning should always be followed (*see* page 5), there are certain techniques that are particular to trees.

Many tree shapes, especially those needing a main leader, can be spoilt if the original leader is lost or dies back – maybe due to frost or disease damage, or if it is broken. In this case, cut back the damaged leader to the nearest strong sideshoot or dormant bud, and tie this shoot to a vertical bamboo cane. On trees with opposite buds, remove the weaker shoot or one of the buds.

Some trees will produce a second competing leader or sideshoot, and these should be removed or shortened to ensure that a main leader, and hence the overall shape of the tree, is maintained.

Some initial training of young trees in their first few years may also be needed to achieve the particular shape and form that is required.

For a central-leader standard, training and pruning should ensure the main stem extends through the crown of the tree; broken leaders and competing leaders are the main problem that may need rectifying.

Branch-headed standards are treated in the same way for the first couple of years, but when three to five strong sideshoots have developed at the desired height of clear trunk, the leader can be pruned back. The selected sideshoots and reduced leader then form the head of the tree.

Feathered trees are the easiest to produce. Simply remove any sideshoots that are not well spaced to produce a balanced tree, and any that have a narrow angle of attachment to the main stem; these may be damaged in strong winds when older and heavier.

Many normally single-stemmed trees can be made into multi-stemmed ones by cutting through the main stem just above ground level or at any required height above it. Select three to five well spaced, strongly developing shoots and remove the rest. Allow all the resulting sideshoots to develop normally, or remove the lowest ones if a clear stem is required.

Naturally weeping standards need staking, and the main stem should be tied in until it reaches the

Initial training of central-leader standard

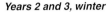

Years 2 and 3, winter

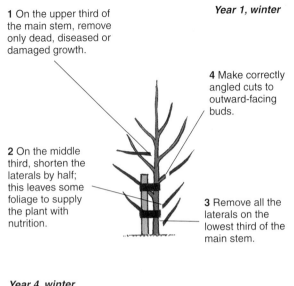

Year 1, winter

1 On the upper third of the main stem, remove only dead, diseased or damaged growth.

4 Make correctly angled cuts to outward-facing buds.

2 On the middle third, shorten the laterals by half; this leaves some foliage to supply the plant with nutrition.

3 Remove all the laterals on the lowest third of the main stem.

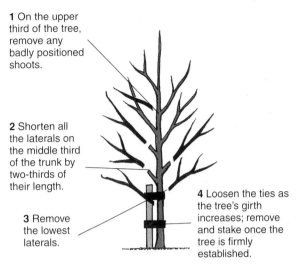

1 On the upper third of the tree, remove any badly positioned shoots.

2 Shorten all the laterals on the middle third of the trunk by two-thirds of their length.

3 Remove the lowest laterals.

4 Loosen the ties as the tree's girth increases; remove and stake once the tree is firmly established.

Year 4, winter

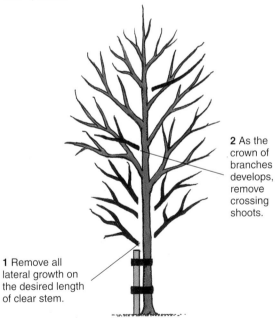

2 As the crown of branches develops, remove crossing shoots.

1 Remove all lateral growth on the desired length of clear stem.

desired height. Branches that grow upwards should be left, as they will eventually take on the natural weeping habit. However, on top-grafted weeping forms, upward stems will continue to grow upwards and should be removed. Any weak growth should also be removed, and any shoots that grow on the clear stem.

Removing Large Branches

This is one area where trees differ from shrubs, in that their larger branches can be difficult to tackle and remove without causing extensive damage to the main trunk or other large branches, and the bark to be badly ripped.

Large pruning cuts may also take several years to heal, and are potential disease entry points that can lead to severe rotting. As a result it is important to make clean cuts with sharp tools, as these heal the most quickly. Rough surfaces must be smoothed with a pruning knife, or in some cases using a chisel can have the desired effect.

It is also important to make the pruning cut in the right place. Large branches should not be cut flush to the stem, rather they should be made so that the branch collar (the ring of swelling at its base) is left intact.

To remove a large branch it may be easier to cut it away in smaller, more manageable sections. Saw through the underside of the branch, or the final section of a large branch, about 30cm (12in) away from the main stem or trunk to about one quarter of its depth; this will prevent any bark tearing should the branch break. Then cut right through the branch from the top a few inches beyond the first undercut. The remaining stub will now be more manageable, and will allow you to carefully make a clean cut following the line of the branch collar. Any rough edges that remain should be smoothed away with a fine saw or pruning knife.

Canopy Issues

Trees with a dense canopy, or whose lower branches are too low, may need more major surgery. Crown lifting – that is, completely removing the lower branches – may be needed to allow free access under the tree. Trees with a dense canopy may need their crown thinned and reduced, whereby branches within the canopy are removed. This may be simply to reduce the amount of shade it casts, or to improve airflow through the tree and so reduce disease.

On large trees both of these are major operations and may be better tackled by a tree surgeon.

TREE SURGEONS

Removing large branches from trees, crown lifting, crown thinning and pollarding, are procedures that are often best left to an expert – a tree surgeon or an arboriculturist.

Locating a qualified, reliable and experienced tree surgeon can often be a problem, and the wrong choice can be both expensive and dangerous.

First, decide on what jobs need doing, as this will help determine whether you need a consultant or a contractor. A consultant will give professional advice on the health and safety of a tree, and will advise on any other issues, including providing guidance in relation to tree preservation orders and planning regulations. A contractor will actually carry out the work.

Always check if there is a charge for preliminary visits, and if this is refundable if work is undertaken. Find out how long they have been in business and what qualifications they have, checking certificates of competence and insurance if necessary. Ask to see references, and even speak to previous clients. Ask more than one contractor for a quote for the work involved, and ensure that this specifies the disposal of surplus material.

The Arboricultural Association has a quality assurance scheme for consultants and contractors: you should contact the Arboricultural Association, Ampfield House, Romsey, Hants SO51 9PA; tel: 01794 368717; website: www.trees.org.uk

Alternatively, contact the tree officer of your local council, who should also be able to supply a list of local experts.

TREE PRESERVATION ORDERS (TPOS)

Some trees, especially those in areas of outstanding natural beauty, may be covered by a tree preservation order (TPO), and it is illegal to carry out any work on them, including pruning, without consulting the issuing body.

TPOs are the legal mechanism to protect and preserve trees for public enjoyment, environmental and aesthetic purposes; bushes, shrubs and hedges are not covered. Trees are also protected by legislation covering Conservation Areas and Sites of Special Scientific Interest.

TPOs are made by the local planning authority (usually the local council) to protect specific trees or a particular woodland from deliberate damage and destruction. They prevent the felling, lopping, topping, uprooting or otherwise wilful damaging of trees without permission. They can be made very quickly, and in practice it is normal for a council to make an emergency TPO in less than a day in cases of immediate danger to trees – although the trees need to be worthy and capable of protection. However, if the case is not urgent it can take many months.

To find out if a tree is protected, contact the local planning authority – usually the local borough or district council.

The full definitive guide to TPO law and practice can be obtained from the government's Communities and Local Government, and is entitled *Tree Preservation Orders: A Guide to the Law and Good Practice*. This is aimed principally at local authorities, and provides detailed guidance on the making, management and enforcement of tree preservation orders. It is available from Communities and Local Government Publications, PO Box

236, Wetherby LS23 7NB; tel: 0870 1226 236; fax: 0870 1226 237; textphone: 0870 1207 405; email: communities@twoten.com; website: www. communities.gov.uk/index.asp?id=1127782

TREES A–Z

Most trees listed here are best grown as a central-leader standard unless otherwise mentioned. The various tree forms are described on page 87. Some trees can also be cut back hard annually to produce a coppiced or pollarded form; this is described on page 19.

Acacia
Mimosa, wattle
Evergreen
Trees or large shrubs grown for their feathery foliage and fragrant yellow flowers produced in winter and spring on the previous year's growth.

Prune young plants after flowering in late spring to a strong sideshoot, or two or three buds beyond the old flower to encourage bushy growth. Remove frost-damaged growth in late spring, but keep any other pruning to a minimum. Young plants of *A. dealbata* may also be cut back by up to half to form a multi-stemmed tree.

Older plants resent hard pruning, and neglected plants can rarely be renovated.

Acer
Maple
Deciduous
Acers are mainly grown for their ornamental foliage – especially their fine autumn colours. Many of the smaller-growing maples produce low branches, which can be encouraged by pruning when young. Species with attractive bark, such as *A. davidii*, *A. griseum* and *A. pensylvanicum*, are grown with clear trunks to show this off, so remove the sideshoots and low branches up to at least 1.5–1.8m (5–6ft).

Acers should be pruned in winter when they are fully dormant, otherwise they bleed sap very heavily, which can weaken the tree. However, very small cuts to remove thin shoots can usually be made in late summer or early autumn.

Otherwise keep pruning to a minimum, apart from removing badly placed or crossing stems and unwanted thin, twiggy growth.

Acer negundo can be pollarded annually to produce a plant with larger leaves and a bushy habit by cutting back branches to a framework.

For pruning shrubby acers, *see* page 30.

Aesculus hippocastrum. (Photo: Tim Sandall)

Aesculus
Horse chestnut, buckeye
Deciduous
Aesculus are grown for their handsome foliage, large candles of white, pink or red flowers produced on the previous year's growth, and their nuts – conkers.

Keep pruning to a minimum; any pruning should be carried out from autumn to mid-winter. Minor pruning to remove thin shoots can also be carried out in summer.

When training young trees, if a shoot leader is lost, it will be replaced by two others; one of these should be removed and the other selected as the new leader.

Shoots that develop around pruning wounds rarely make suitable replacement branches and are best removed.

A. parviflora is a large suckering shrub forming a dense growth of branches. If this becomes too thick it should be pruned out in winter.

Ailanthus

Tree of heaven
Deciduous

This upright tree is grown for its bold foliage, attractive bark and reddish fruits, produced on female plants.

Keep pruning to a minimum; any pruning should be carried out in spring. If the central leader is lost, the resulting regrowth should be thinned out but the plant allowed to develop as a multi-stemmed tree.

Ailanthus is a tall tree, but can be grown as a shrub by coppicing every year, or every other.

Alnus

Alder
Deciduous

Alders are grown for their attractive foliage, and for their catkins produced in late winter or early spring. They are tolerant of a wide range of soil conditions, so are often grown where conditions aren't suitable for other species.

Although alders are usually grown as a central-leader standard, the natural development of some species, such as *A. glutinosa*, *A. incana* and *A. japonica*, is as multi-stemmed trees. If these are to be grown as standards, select and train a single stem.

Established trees don't require regular pruning, but unwanted stems can be removed from autumn until mid-winter. Making minor cuts to remove small shoots can be done in summer.

Betula pendula (silver birch). *(Photo: Tim Sandall)*

Betula

Birch
Deciduous

Birches are grown for their graceful habit, autumn colour and attractive peeling bark.

They should be pruned from autumn to winter when they are fully dormant, otherwise they bleed sap very heavily, which can weaken them.

Upright spreading trees, such as *B. albosinensis*, *B. ermanii*, *B. nigra*, *B. papyrifera* and *B. utilis*, can be trained as central-leader standards or as feathered trees. Once they are established they need little pruning apart from removing unwanted main branches, weak twiggy growth, and anything that obscures the bark.

The common *B. pendula* is a semi-weeping tree that spreads with age and can be grown as a central-leader standard, a feathered tree or a multi-stemmed tree.

Weeping birches should be grown as weeping standards. Such trees can become very wide with age, and excessive growth is best removed before the tree becomes top heavy.

The hard pruning of most birches is not recommended.

Carpinus
Hornbeam
Deciduous
Hornbeam is grown for its catkins in spring, its attractive autumnal foliage colours, and its silvered bark in winter.

Pruning should be carried out from late summer until mid-winter as pruning at other times can lead to severe bleeding.

Carpinus can be grown as a central-leader standard, as a feathered tree or pleached.

Established trees need little in the way of pruning. Neglected trees will tolerate heavy pruning, but the resulting mass of thin growth is not suitable for maintaining a tree unless it is severely thinned.

Castanea
Chestnut
Deciduous
These summer-flowering trees produce spiny fruits and sometimes edible nuts. The species most widely grown is *C. sativa*, the sweet chestnut.

Pruning should be carried out when dormant, in autumn and winter, although minor pruning can be done in late summer.

Train standard plants with evenly, well spaced, wide V-angled sideshoots coming from the main stem. Established trees need little in the way of pruning, although it can be a good idea to reduce the spread of mature branches by shortening them to prevent wind damage.

Catalpa
Bean tree
Deciduous
A very ornamental tree producing large, handsome leaves, purplish-pink or white flowers in summer followed by long, dark brown seedpods that persist well into the winter. *C. bignonioides* 'Aurea' has golden leaves and is the cultivar most commonly grown.

Pruning should be carried out when dormant, from autumn to late winter; frost-damaged growth can be removed in mid- to late spring. Train as a central-leader standard with well-spaced sideshoots or as a branch-headed standard.

Established trees need little pruning, but old, long, heavy branches may need to be shortened or removed to balance the framework and prevent them from being damaged by winter storms.

Catalpa responds well to hard pruning, and *C. bignonioides* 'Aurea' is best treated this way to increase the size and quality of its foliage. It can also be pollarded by cutting back branches every year or every other year in late winter.

Cercidiphyllum japonicum
Katsura tree
Deciduous
This graceful tree has heart-shaped leaves that have excellent autumn colour and scent, smelling like candyfloss or burnt sugar.

A tree will either grow with a single central leader, or produce a multi-stemmed effect, and each will grow in its own preferred way: don't try to change it or prune it into a different form.

Multi-stemmed trees branch at an early age and need no formative pruning, although excessive and weak stems can be removed in autumn or winter when dormant. Any dead and frost-damaged growth can be removed in spring. Single-leader trees may need the lower branches removing to form a clear stem when dormant.

Established trees need little or no pruning. Neglected trees do not respond well to hard pruning.

Cercis
Judas tree, redbud
Deciduous
Cercis is grown for its pink or white pea-like spring flowers formed on older wood and appearing before, or as the foliage emerges; the latter produces excellent autumn tints. *C. canadensis*

Cercis canadensis 'Forest Pansy'. *(Photo: Tim Sandall)*

'Forest Pansy' is a popular form that produces purple leaves. Prune all *Cercis* in early summer.

They are usually grown as multi-stemmed trees or shrubs with a framework of three to five well-spaced stems, thinning out any that are not needed.

Established trees need no pruning. Old, neglected trees can usually be renovated by cutting back to just above ground level and selecting up to five young framework branches.

C. canadensis can also be grown as a feathered tree or on a 90cm (3ft) stem.

Cornus
Tree dogwood, cornel
Deciduous
There are a number of *Cornus* species that are grown as trees. These are grown for their large, colourful bracts surrounding the small summer flowers, also for their form and their foliage. They should be pruned from autumn to early spring and generally don't tolerate hard pruning.

C. alternifolia and *C. controversa* are trained as a central-leader standard, where pruning consists of removing competing leaders and low sideshoots in the first two or three years; they need little in the way of pruning afterwards. *C. alternifolia* can also be grown as a multi-stemmed, feathered tree.

C. florida and *C. kousa* are best grown on a short leg, up to 90cm (3ft) long, by removing all sideshoots to this height. Thereafter they are best left to their own devices.

For pruning shrubby *Cornus*, *see* page 36.

Corylus colurna
Turkish hazel
Deciduous
Corylus colurna has an upright habit and produces male catkins in winter and early spring on branches covered in a shaggy bark. The tiny female flowers provide a red haze on the branches.

Remove any competing leaders to ensure the tree retains a single leader. Established trees need little in the way of pruning, but neglected trees respond well to being pruned hard if necessary. All pruning should be carried out in winter when the tree is dormant.

For pruning shrubby hazels, *see* page 37; for pruning cobnuts and filberts, *see* page 130.

Crataegus
Thorn trees
Deciduous
The common hawthorn, or May tree, is a spectacular sight in spring, covered in white, pink or sometimes red flowers. These are often followed in autumn by mainly orange or red fruit (haws). All thorn trees can be pruned at any time from autumn and early spring.

The common hawthorn, *C. monogyna*, *C. laevigata*, their cultivars and the less common *C. tanacetifolia*, can be grown as a central-leader or branch-headed standard or as a multi-stemmed tree.

Established trees need little in the way of further pruning, although congestion in the crown is common and you may want to thin out overcrowded and rubbing branches – but don't overdo it.

C. crus-galli and *C. persimilis* 'Prunifolia' produce strong leaders and make good branch-headed standards.

Davidia
Handkerchief tree
Deciduous
A stately tree with graceful, hanging white bracts produced from late spring on the previous year's growth.

Trees naturally form a strong central leader, with strong upright sideshoots. These may overtake the leader, so should be removed gradually, reduced, or removed from autumn to early spring until there is a clear stem of the desired height.

Established trees usually need no regular attention; they do not respond to hard pruning, and are reluctant to re-shoot.

Embothrium
Chilean firebush
Evergreen
Embothrium is sometimes semi-evergreen in harsh winters, and bears masses of bright red flowers along the stems of the previous year's growth in late spring or early summer.

Its suckering habit lends it to be growing as a multi-stemmed tree, or it can be grown with a central leader. It is best left to grow unchecked with little or no pruning, apart from removing misshapen and unwanted growth; those grown as multi-stemmed trees should have some stems thinned out to ground level to avoid overcrowding. Pruning should be carried out in late summer after flowering. Any winter-damaged growth can be removed in spring.

Eucalyptus
Gum tree
Evergreen
The gum trees are grown for their attractive, aromatic evergreen foliage and, in some species, peeling bark in colours ranging from cream, green and grey-pink. Many species produce juvenile and adult foliage that is very different in its shape and often colour. Pruning should be carried out in spring after the risk of hard frosts has passed.

They are trained as central-leader standards, although the leader may lose its dominance as the tree matures, to produce a multi-branched effect. Some species naturally form multi-stemmed trees. All can be hard pruned, even cut back to a stump just above ground level if they are damaged; they will reshoot to form a thicket of shoots that can be thinned out, if a single-stemmed tree is needed, or left as they are. Some, such as *E. gunnii* and *E. pauciflora* subsp. *niphophila*, are grown as pollarded or coppiced shrubs (*see* page 19 for details) as

Eucalyptus dalrympleana. (Photo: Tim Sandall)

regular pruning maintains the more attractive juvenile foliage.

Most gum trees have a weak root system, which can cause them to topple when mature during strong winds. Because of this, in windy areas it is often better to grow them as shorter, multi-stemmed trees.

Eucryphia
Evergreen
Eucryphia is grown for its glossy foliage and white flowers in summer.

It does not need, or like, much pruning and does not respond to hard pruning. It is best left to its own devices.

Shoots that have been damaged by winter cold or strong winds can be cut back in spring to just above a suitable sideshoot. If possible, try and reduce all other branches to the same height.

Fagus
Beech
Deciduous

The common beech, *Fagus sylvatica*, is a stately, large tree with a dense crown grown mainly for its foliage. As it can reach great heights, up to 30m (100ft), it is usually only grown in large gardens or parks. Pruning should be carried out from autumn to early spring.

Initially, plants should be trained as feathered trees to promote a strong leader and ensure stable root growth, otherwise trees can become unstable in future years.

After a few years the sideshoots produced low down on the main stem can be cleared to form the main trunk; this should be done over several years and not all in one go. As the crown develops, remove any competing leaders. Established trees rarely need any further formative pruning.

The weeping cultivar, *F. sylvatica* 'Pendula', should be trained up a stake until the required height is reached, and then the head allowed to form. Clearing shoots from the main stem will produce a standard weeping plant, but they can be left in place where they will root on touching the ground to form a very widely spreading plant.

Fraxinus
Ash
Deciduous

Ashes are mainly grown for their ornamental foliage, although a few, such as *F. ornus*, also have attractive spring flowers.

Ashes usually require little formative pruning as they naturally produce a central leader and subsequent crown. Mature trees need little pruning apart from removing damaged branches and water shoots that form around damaged growth. Pruning should be carried out when the tree is dormant, between autumn and early spring.

F. angustifolia 'Raywood' can be grown as a central-leader standard or as a feathered tree.

Fraxinus ornus. (Photo: Tim Sandall)

The weeping ash, *F. excelsior* 'Pendula', is grown as a weeping standard, and should only be lightly pruned to remove crossing branches and an even spacing of branches.

Ash trees do not respond well to hard pruning.

Gleditsia
Honey locust
Deciduous

Gleditsia is grown for its elegant habit and its foliage that often turns yellow in the autumn. The golden form, *G. triacanthos* 'Sunburst', is the one most commonly grown.

Trees rarely need formative training and pruning, and even mature trees can be left to their own devices, apart from removing dead or damaged wood in spring. Any other pruning should be carried out from late summer to early winter.

Juglans

Walnut

Deciduous

Apart from *J. regia*, which is mainly grown for its walnuts, *J. nigra* is grown as an ornamental tree for its large leaves and beautiful bark. It has a pyramidal shape when young, but spreads wider as it matures.

It is important to remove sideshoots from the trunk when the tree is young to reduce blemishes and cavities. Pruning is best kept to a minimum on established trees, and any pruning must be carried out from mid-summer to early autumn; pruning in late winter or spring can cause severe bleeding. Trees do not respond well to hard pruning.

For pruning fruiting walnuts, *see* page 130.

Koelreuteria

Deciduous

Koelreuteria is grown for its finely divided foliage, yellow flowers in mid- to late summer, and butter-yellow autumn foliage tints.

Sadly this is a weak, often short-lived tree. Keep pruning to a minimum, do not tip-prune to encourage bushy growth, and certainly don't hard prune. Any pruning simply to remove dead, damaged and dying-back growth is best carried out in winter when dormant.

Laburnum

Golden chain, golden rain

Deciduous

A tree for providing a splash of colour, producing lots of long pendent yellow flowers in late spring and early summer. Pruning is best carried out from late summer to late autumn.

It can be grown as a feathered tree or a central-leader standard; the latter will show off the flowers to full advantage. Prune shoots when they are young, as removing large branches can lead to cavities and disease problems. Aim not to prune established trees apart from spur pruning to promote flowering – that is, cutting back sideshoots to two or three leaves or buds. Laburnums do not respond well to hard pruning, and rarely survive renovation.

The weeping *L. alpinum* and *L. anagyroides* 'Pendulum' are grown as top-grafted weeping standards.

Laburnums respond well to training and regular pruning, and can be pleached or made into laburnum walks or arches.

It is a good idea to remove the seedpods, especially if you have children, as the seeds are poisonous.

Laurus

Bay, sweet bay, bay laurel

Evergreen

Bay is grown for its aromatic foliage much prized in cooking. In cool climates the foliage may become damaged during cold winters.

It grows naturally as a central-leader tree, or can be trained as a feathered tree, or treated as a shrub and pruned and trained as a rounded bush, pyramid or lollipop standard. Pruning should be carried out in spring, just as new growth begins; light trimming and shaping can also be done in summer.

For pruning hedges, *see* page 111.

Liquidambar styraciflua 'Worplesdon'.
(Photo: Tim Sandall)

Liquidambar

Sweet gum

Deciduous

These stately trees are grown for their superb autumn leaf colour.

Grown as a central-leader standard, competing leaders must be removed as soon as they're seen.

Little or no pruning is needed apart from removing unwanted branches, and this should be done any time from late autumn to early spring; dead wood can also be removed in late summer.

Liriodendron

Tulip tree
Deciduous

The stately tulip tree has attractive foliage that turns golden in autumn, and pale green, tulip-like flowers in mid-summer.

Little, if any, formative pruning is needed, and pruning of established trees should be kept to a minimum as wood rot is quite common. If pruning is needed it should be done from autumn to early spring, although dead wood can be removed when the tree is in full leaf. Always use sharp tools and make very clean cuts.

Magnolia

Deciduous and evergreen

Although most magnolias are classed as shrubs, one or two species are tree-like in their growth. The general principles of pruning are the same: *see* page 47 for details.

M. campbellii and *M. kobus* produce pyramidal trees with a strong central leader. Any pruning should be carried out in summer. Only prune out competing leaders and damaged growth; hard pruning produces vertical shoots that spoil the overall shape. As the plant matures, lower branches can be removed over a number of years if required, otherwise no further pruning is usually needed. *M. kobus* may produce water shoots, which should be removed as soon as they are noticed.

Old, neglected plants may be successfully renovated by pruning back all the branches to the main framework, but this should be done over a three-year period.

M. delavayi, *M. denudata* and *M. grandiflora*, when grown as a tree, are similar, but often produce long, thin branches that can spoil the shape. These should be pruned back in spring as growth begins.

For pruning shrubby magnolias, *see* page 47; for pruning *Magnolia grandiflora* as a wall shrub, *see* page 72.

Malus 'White Star'. *(Photo: Tim Sandall)*

Malus

Crab apple
Deciduous

Crab apples are highly ornamental, being grown for their flowers, fruit and foliage. There are many small forms that are perfect for even the smallest garden.

They are grown as standards, and once the framework branches are formed, little formative pruning is needed. Future pruning usually only consists of removing badly placed or crossing branches, water shoots that form in the crown, and any inward-growing shoots that produce a congested habit. Pruning can be carried out at any time from autumn to early spring.

Crab apples do not respond well to hard pruning.

For pruning apples, *see* page 123.

Morus alba

White mulberry
Deciduous

The white mulberry is grown for its ornamental growth habit, and its attractive bark and fruit. Although the latter is edible, it tastes insipid, and the black mulberry, *Morus nigra* and its cultivars, is best for quality edible fruit.

Help maintain the central leader for as long as possible, or train in a replacement if it fails. As the tree matures, the uppermost sideshoots will naturally overtake the leader to form a broad-headed tree. There is no need to worry about this, and in fact pruning is best kept to a minimum. Too much pruning, especially renovation pruning, can lead to an excessive production of water shoots, which affect subsequent growth and need thinning out. Any pruning that is needed should be carried out in autumn or early winter when fully dormant to prevent sap bleeding.

M. alba 'Pendula' is a popular weeping cultivar. It needs training and tying into a stout support until the desired height is reached. Each winter, gradually remove sideshoots from the bottom 1.5–1.8m (5–6ft) of the main stem. After that the crown can be allowed to develop and weep naturally; keep pruning to a minimum, just removing damaged and very weak growth.

For pruning *Morus nigra*, the black mulberry, *see* page 129.

Nothofagus
Southern beech
Deciduous and evergreen
These beeches are fine, large trees often grown in parks; they produce finely textured foliage, and the deciduous species usually produce excellent autumn leaf tints.

The evergreen species tend to produce dual leaders, which can cause problems at maturity, so remove the weakest at the earliest opportunity. Established trees need no regular pruning, but lower branches may grow to ground level and restrict access underneath the tree; if this is a problem they should be removed. All pruning should be carried out in late spring.

With deciduous species it is also important to maintain a single strong leader, and lower branches may need to be removed, too. Pruning should be carried out from autumn to early spring.

Nyssa
Tupelo, sour gum
Deciduous
Nyssas are grown for their stately habit and attractive foliage, especially in autumn when it takes on fiery colours.

In cool climates trees often lose their leader and grow as multi-stemmed trees with a framework of branches on a short trunk (or leg). In warmer climates they can be grown as central-leader trees.

All pruning should be carried out when the tree is dormant, from late autumn until early spring.

In cool climates it is often best to tip-prune after planting to encourage the multi-stem effect; then select four to six of the strongest resulting branches to form the framework. Sideshoots from the leg can be removed to give a clear trunk. Little further pruning is needed.

To grow as a central-leader standard, remove the main sideshoots gradually, starting in the second year after planting. Hard pruning early in the tree's life can result in early branching in the crown, which can ruin the overall look.

Oxydendrum
Sorrel tree
Deciduous
The sorrel tree is grown for its greenish-white flowers in summer and brilliant red autumn colour.

In warm areas it tends to grow only as a single-leader tree; elsewhere it develops as a multi-stemmed tree or even as a bush. Pruning is best kept to a minimum, but unwanted branches and excessive growth can be removed when the plant is dormant, from autumn to early spring.

Parrotia persica. (Photo: Tim Sandall)

Parrotia persica
Persian ironwood
Deciduous
The Persian ironwood is mainly grown for its colourful autumn leaf tints, but also for its attractive bark.

Plants either develop a central leader and can be grown as a tree, or, in some cases, this leader is lost and the plant develops a shrubby habit with lots of sideshoots with a horizontal or hanging habit.

Both types develop naturally, with little or no formative pruning, and should be allowed to grow in whichever way they take. Established trees can also be left to get on with things; unwanted and damaged growth can be removed at any time from autumn to early spring.

Paulownia
Foxglove tree
Deciduous
Paulownia is grown for its handsome foliage and foxglove-like spring flowers. A long, hot summer is needed to ripen the wood to produce flower buds in the autumn, but these may drop off during cold winter weather. As a result, it is often better to grow *Paulownia* as a coppiced or pollarded shrub for its foliage, and to prune to encourage this. All pruning should be carried out from mid-spring to early summer.

If growing as a central-leader standard, try to rub out the buds that appear on the lower 1.2–1.5 (4–5ft) of stem, rather than pruning out the subsequent branches. Further pruning should be to remove damaged and unwanted growth.

The leader may easily be lost, and the crown may start to branch early. In warm areas it should be possible to replace the leader with a vigorous sideshoot. In colder regions numerous sideshoots develop, resulting in a shrubby, multi-stemmed effect; in this case, prune back hard annually to make a pollarded or coppiced plant. This pruning encourages the leaves to grow much larger, and produces an excellent foliage effect.

Platanus
Plane
Deciduous
These large, stately trees produce attractive bark and, if left unpruned, graceful branches that sweep to the ground. They grow too big for most gardens, but can be hard pruned and are often pollarded annually. Pruning should be carried out from autumn to early spring.

You can either clear the main trunk up to a height of 2.4–3m (8–10ft) or, to have branches down to ground level, remove sideshoots to 1.2m (4ft) and prune remaining sideshoots to downward-facing buds. Strong, upright shoots should be removed or they can compete with the main leader.

P. orientalis often produces too many sideshoots, and some should be removed to leave only evenly spaced branches. In later years crown thinning and reduction may be needed to prevent the head becoming too congested.

Populus
Poplar
Deciduous
These are fast-growing trees grown for their stature; they are usually too big for most gardens, and are often used as a windbreak. They should be pruned in late summer or early autumn; they will bleed if pruned in late winter or early spring.

Most are grown as central-leader standards with well spaced sideshoots, although *P. nigra* var. *italica*, the Italian poplar, is grown as a feathered tree whose young sideshoots can be shortened to produce bushier growth. No regular pruning is needed. Generally, they do not respond well to hard pruning.

P. × jackii 'Aurora' (often sold as *P. × candicans* 'Aurora') is grown as a central-leader or branch-headed standard, but can be grown as a coppiced or pollarded, multi-stemmed shrub, especially in small gardens. Coppicing helps encourage its attractive, cream-blotched leaves.

Prunus
Ornamental cherry
Deciduous
The ornamental cherries are a large and diverse group of trees grown for various different attributes: their foliage, in particular their autumn tints, also their flowers, fruit and attractive bark.

Pruning should be kept to an absolute minimum and always carried out in summer; pruning at other times can encourage diseases such as silver leaf and bacterial canker, which will damage the tree and even lead to its eventual death. If formative pruning is necessary it should be done as soon

Prunus 'Shirofugen' (flowering cherry).
(Photo: Tim Sandall)

P. calleryana, the willow-leaved pear *P. salicifolia*, and its widely available weeping cultivar 'Pendula', are grown with a clear stem of around 1.5–1.6m (5–6ft), although the species can be left with shoots intact to provide foliage to the ground. Sideshoots in the head should be thinned out at an early age to create an evenly spaced and balanced framework of branches. Established trees don't need further pruning, but light trimming or the removal of young, unwanted branches can be carried out. Plants don't respond well to hard pruning.

For pruning fruiting pears, *see* page 126.

as possible, and all pruning wounds should be made as small as possible; large wounds are perfect sites for disease entry. Established trees usually need little in the way of pruning, and prefer not to be pruned. They don't usually respond well to hard pruning.

The species cherries are usually grown as a central-leader standard with evenly spaced sideshoots. Those grown for their attractive bark, such as *P. serrula*, should have the young shoots and branches that form on the main trunk removed or rubbed out at an early age in order to show off the bark to its best advantage. The various cultivars of Japanese flowering cherries vary in their growth habits, and are grown as either central-leader, branch-headed or weeping standards; they need little, if any pruning.

For pruning fruiting cherries, *see* page 126.

Pyrus
Ornamental pear
Deciduous

Ornamental pears produce masses of white blossom in spring, followed by small fruit, and in some species attractive foliage, including good autumn colours.

Pruning should be carried out from autumn to early spring.

Quercus robur f. fastigiata. (Photo: Tim Sandall)

Quercus
Oak
Deciduous and evergreen
These are large, stately trees usually too big for all but the largest garden. Train them as a central-leader standard with even and well spaced sideshoots to ensure a good shape to the crown. Established plants need little in the way of pruning, which, if needed, can be carried out between autumn and early spring.

Q. ilex, the evergreen holm oak, looks shrubby when young and should be trained as a feathered tree. It does produce a central leader, and lower branches are shed naturally to produce a single-stemmed tree.

Pruning should be restricted to dealing with damaged growth, and trimming winter-damaged shoots; it should be carried out in summer.

Robinia
False acacia
Deciduous
Robinias are grown mainly for their ornamental foliage, but they do produce flowers, and some have attractive bark. The wood is brittle, and trees can shed even large branches in windy weather; however, good initial training can reduce this risk. All pruning should be carried out in summer.

It is important to maintain the main leader for as long as possible into the tree's early life, so all competing leaders must be removed as early as possible. Ensure that all main sideshoots are evenly and well spaced, and remove upright growth that appears close to the main trunk.

The pruning of established trees is best kept to a minimum, and large cuts are prone to rotting. However, damaged and small, unwanted branches can be removed.

Salix
Willow
Deciduous
The tree willows are generally tall, and are often spreading plants, only suitable for large gardens or open spaces. They are grown for their graceful habit, especially the weeping types, and for their spring catkins, stem colour and foliage. Pruning can be carried out at any time from autumn to early spring.

The weeping Kilmarnock willow, *S. caprea* 'Kilmarnock', is a small tree that forms an umbrella-shaped canopy of stiffly weeping branches. Although they need little formative pruning apart from removing unwanted stems, they do need annual pruning after a few years to prevent the crown from becoming congested. This should be done as the catkins fade. The aim should be to remove about half of the stems from the middle of the crown, and any wayward ones growing in the wrong direction or increasing the width of the plant unnecessarily.

For pruning shrubby willows, *see* page 54.

Sophora
Deciduous
Sophoras are grown for their ornamental foliage, pendant flowers and, in some species, their attractive bark.

In warm climates they naturally produce a central leader and form a good branch system, and need little formative pruning. In cooler regions, the central leader is often lost and a heavy head of branches forms. These may be damaged and break in strong winds, so it is important to maintain the central leader for as long as possible, and to select sideshoots that will form a good, balanced framework of branches. If the leader is lost, try and select a sideshoot as a replacement.

Any pruning should be carried out in summer, as pruning in winter or spring can lead to severe bleeding. Established trees need little pruning and don't respond well to hard pruning and renovation.

Sorbus
Mountain ash, rowan, whitebeam
Deciduous
A versatile group of trees grown for their form, attractive foliage, flowers, fruit and, in some species, excellent autumn leaf colours. They generally need little in the way of pruning, but any that is needed should be carried out from autumn to early spring; dead wood can be removed in summer.

Once the single leader with five or six evenly and well-spaced sideshoots has been trained and formed, there is little else that needs to be done. Restrict further pruning to the removal of damaged and crossing branches.

Styrax
Deciduous and evergreen
These trees, or large shrubs, are grown for their graceful habit and hanging clusters of white flowers in summer.

They dislike being pruned, and are best left to develop naturally. As the crown develops, lower branches may die back and should be removed at any time from autumn to early spring. Established trees rarely need any further pruning, and don't respond to hard pruning.

S. hemsleyanus and *S. obassia* are usually best grown as multi-stemmed trees, but hard pruning can lead to vigorous regrowth that may be damaged in winter.

Tilia
Lime, linden
Deciduous
Tilias are large trees grown for their stature, form, foliage and sweetly scented flowers. Pruning should be carried out from midsummer to early winter; they will bleed if pruned in spring.

They are grown as central-leader standards, ensuring there are even and well spaced sideshoots to produce a balanced crown. Several species produce lots of water shoots along their stems, and these are best removed as they can spoil the shape of the crown if allowed to develop. Mature trees generally don't respond well to hard, renovation pruning.

When mature, some species produce dense crowns, often containing a lot of dead wood; some of this may even be dropped from the tree. Limes are tolerant of pruning and can be pollarded. They are also perfectly suited to pleaching.

Ulmus
Elm
Deciduous
Generally, elms are large stately trees grown for their stature and form.

Most are grown as central-leader standards, although *U. parvifolia* and *U. pumila* are best left to grow without training and pruning. When growing standards, ensure the sideshoots are even and well spaced, removing any that are not, and tip-pruning any that compete with the leader.

Established trees need little, if any pruning, although some species, especially *U. procera*, are strangely prone to branch drop in summer, and overlong, weak branches may need to be removed. Pruning should be carried out from autumn to early spring.

Zelkova
Deciduous
Zelkova is grown for its colourful autumn leaf tints and attractive bark.

Train as a central-leader standard with a well spaced framework of branches. Lower branches may need to be removed to allow access underneath the tree; any pruning should be done in late winter. In the early years, tip back branches to a suitable sideshoot when in full leaf in summer to encourage branching and upright growth.

Pruning Calendar

	spring	summer	autumn	winter
Acacia	■ ■			
Acer		■ (light cuts only)	■ (light cuts only)	■ ■ ■
Aesculus		■ ■ ■ (light cuts only)	■ ■ ■	■ ■
Ailanthus	■ ■ ■			
Alnus		■ ■ ■ (light cuts only)	■ ■ ■	■ ■
Betula	■	■ ■ (light cuts only)	■ ■ ■	■ ■ ■
Carpinus	■ ■		■ ■ ■	■ ■
Castanea		(light cuts only)	■ ■ ■ ■	■ ■ ■
Catalpa	■ ■ (removal of frost damage)		■ ■ ■	■ ■ ■
Cercidiphyllum japonicum	■ ■ ■ (removal of frost damage)		■ ■ ■	■ ■ ■
Cercis		■		
Cornus	■		■ ■ ■	■ ■ ■
Corylus colurna				■ ■ ■
Crataegus	■		■ ■ ■	■ ■ ■
Davidia	■		■ ■ ■	■ ■ ■
Embothrium	■	■		
Eucalyptus	■ ■			
Eucryphia	■ ■ ■			
Fagus	■		■ ■ ■	■ ■ ■
Fraxinus	■		■ ■ ■	■ ■ ■
Gleditsia	■ ■ ■			
Juglans		■ ■	■ ■ ■	
Koelreuteria				■ ■ ■
Laburnum		■	■ ■ ■	
Liquidambar	■		■ ■ ■	■ ■ ■
Liriodendron	■		■ ■ ■	■ ■ ■

	spring			summer			autumn			winter		
Magnolia	■	■	■	■	■	■						
Malus	■						■	■	■	■	■	■
Morus alba							■	■	■	■		
Nothofagus												
Evergreen			■									
Deciduous	■						■	■	■	■	■	■
Nyssa	■							■	■	■	■	■
Oxydendrum	■						■	■	■	■	■	■
Parrotia persica	■						■	■	■	■	■	■
Paulownia		■	■	■								
Platanus	■						■	■	■	■	■	■
Populus						■	■					
Prunus				■	■	■						
Pyrus	■						■	■	■	■	■	■
Quercus	■						■	■	■	■	■	■
Robinia				■	■	■						
Salix	■						■	■	■	■	■	■
Sophora				■	■	■						
Sorbus	■						■	■	■	■	■	■
Styrax	■						■	■	■	■	■	■
Tilia					■	■	■	■	■	■		
Ulmus	■						■	■	■	■	■	■
Zelkova												■

Each season divided into three – to represent the three months that make up that season

■ = pruning time

CONIFERS

Sadly for most garden conifers, they are usually only given attention and pruned when it is too late – when they have already got too big, spread too far, produced extensive dead areas or generally outgrown their allotted position. And it is sad, because the majority of conifers will not reshoot from old wood, and hard pruning into such old, brown growth causes dead patches at best and complete dieback of that part of the plant at worst.

When choosing conifers, always take into account their growth rate (the heights given on plant labels are usually a ten-year height – they'll grow more or less the same rate in the next ten years!) and the situation you're growing them in; conifers for rockeries and for growing close to the house need careful selection.

Pruning is best avoided on mature plants, unless absolutely essential – such as to remove reverted, wayward, dead or damaged growth – and then should be carried out in such a way that only young, green growth is removed. If a branch has died back completely this should be removed and nearby shoots trained and tied in to cover the bare area if possible. With pines, spruces, cedars and other conifers that produce whorls of branches from the main stem, removing a single branch may produce lopsided growth. In which case, and if the damage is on the lowest whorl of branches, you may want to remove the lowest whorl completely.

Mature conifers that have grown too tall and have their growing point and some top growth removed usually grow outwards producing a badly shaped, top-heavy, broad-spreading, ugly plant.

Conifers with splayed-out growth, perhaps as a result of wind damage, snow loading or just the weight of an upright branch, are best treated by tying in the wayward growth rather than removing it. Providing the shoot isn't damaged, carefully bring it back to its original position and tie it in place with soft string.

Many conifers, especially *Chamaecyparis*, *Cupressus*, *Juniperus* and *Thuja* species and cultivars, can accumulate dead branches and leaves within their outer growth. If necessary this can be cleared out, providing it is done carefully and without damaging the external appearance of the plant.

Initial Training

Young plants will usually benefit from some initial training and pruning. Most conifers naturally produce a central leader to ensure upright growth or sideways growth in the case of prostrate and semi-prostrate cultivars. If damage to the central shoot occurs in early life it may be naturally replaced. If not, or if damage occurs later on, you may need to retrain a leader to replace it. This is easily done by cutting back the damaged growth to a strong shoot, inserting a cane through the plant and tying it to the main stem, then carefully tying in the new replacement shoot to the cane.

Some conifers, however, may produce dual leaders in response to damage. In such cases the weaker or more crooked leader should be removed.

HARD PRUNING

The following conifers usually respond well to hard pruning:

Cryptomeria
Cunninghamia
Sequoia
Taxus

The following can be hard pruned if necessary when very young:

Araucaria
Metasequoia
Taxodium

For pruning hedging conifers, *see* page 109.

PALMS AND PALM-LIKE PLANTS

Palms are great plants for those gardeners who hate pruning or mistrust their pruning skills, as they need minimal training and hardly any or no pruning. One possible exception is the Chusan palm, *Trachycarpus fortunei*, whose leaves can remain on the main trunk until they reach down to the ground, making them look less attractive. In this case the leaves may be removed from the lower branches.

Wear stout gloves if and when you do have to do any pruning, as many palms produce spiky leaves or spiny leaf bases.

True palms and palm-like plants (such as aloes, agaves, cordylines, phormiums and yuccas) do benefit from an annual tidying up in mid- to late spring or summer to removed dead or damaged leaves. For most palms this consists of cutting them off neatly about 5–8cm (2–3in) from the trunk, ensuring that the remaining stubs produce a neat, 'groomed' appearance. Don't cut them back right to the stem, as this can look unattractive and makes the stem more susceptible to damage. Damaged leaves are best left until they have dried out and become shrivelled.

The dead leaves of cordylines, phormiums and yuccas are best removed completely by carefully pulling them away. If they don't come away cleanly and easily in your hands, leave them to dry out further or cut them off with secateurs.

Some palms produce a fibrous, protective covering on the trunk which is best left alone to prevent any possible damage. It tends to be shed naturally as the plant matures.

The spent flower spikes are best removed too, wherever this is feasible. You should cut back the flowered stem as far as possible to their point of origin, aiming not to leave behind any dead stem.

It is not possible to restrict the size of most true palms, because if the growing tip is removed they will die. They don't have growth buds lower down on the stem. The height and spread of suckering palms, such as *Chamaerops*, can be controlled by completely removing the tallest trunk and/or widely spaced suckers.

Most palm-like plants, on the other hand, don't produce all their growth from a single growing point and do have buds lower down on the stem. As a result they can be hard pruned to reduce their size or to remove completely damaged heads. Usually more than one bud will break, producing a multi-headed effect. They even respond well to renovation pruning, cutting them back to side or basal shoots, or even to just above ground level.

The rosette-forming agaves and aloes readily produce new rosettes. Damaged or large rosettes can be carefully removed, ensuring there is no injury to the new shoots growing below.

CHAPTER 8

Hedges

A hedge is the most natural boundary around your garden that you can have. It's a living, growing entity which, if cared for, will look beautiful and still do what it's meant to do: be a thick, impenetrable screen or barrier to provide privacy and security, hide an eyesore, act as a windbreak, or even be a noise filter. Most can also provide food, shelter and nesting sites for wildlife.

Of course, hedges don't have to be massive and only grown around the perimeter of the garden: they can be used throughout the garden to help break it up into smaller sections or 'rooms', and dwarf hedges can be used to edge paths, beds and borders.

The choice of plants is almost without limit, the only proviso being that it is something that tolerates pruning! Then choose the size, type and style of hedge you want, whether a dense, formal evergreen conifer hedge, an informal deciduous flowering hedge, a wildlife hedge, or a thorny security hedge.

INITIAL TRAINING

A hedge is a long-term feature, so it needs to be planted correctly in well-prepared soil, and cared for from the start. The planting distance apart depends on the vigour of the species chosen; most are planted 38–60cm (15–24in) apart, although vigorous conifers such as × *Cupressocyparis leylandii* can be planted 75–90cm (2½–3ft) apart. And even though you probably want the hedge to grow as tall and bushy as possible as soon as possible, you

*OPPOSITE: A hedge of Ligustrum ovalifolium 'Aureum'.
(Photo: Tim Sandall)*

should prune after planting to ensure bushy growth. It's usually difficult to make something of a poor hedge, so start as you mean to go on!

The amount of pruning depends on the plants chosen and the effect required. Flowering shrubs used for informal hedges should be pruned lightly, as recommended for a free-standing specimen (*see* the shrub section, starting on page 30, and the tree section starting on page 91). Most evergreens need minimal pruning, shortening just the overlong sideshoots; don't prune the main shoot (leader) until the desired height has been reached, especially if you're using conifers. When training conifer hedges it is usually best to allow the plants to grow 15cm (6in) above the desired height and then remove the top 30cm (12in) of growth; this way you'll hide the unsightly cut leader.

Beech and hornbeam need moderate pruning to stimulate bushy growth; to even up unbalanced growth, prune strong shoots lightly and weak ones hard. Shorten very vigorous leaders and sideshoots by no more than one-third, the weaker ones by two-thirds.

Vigorous plants with an upright habit, such as hawthorn, privet and snowberry, need harder pruning to encourage bushy growth. Cut them back to within 15–30cm (6–12in) of the ground, and cut back sideshoots in summer. In the second winter, prune hard again to remove about half of the previous year's growth.

WHICH HEDGING PLANT?

There are two basic types of hedge: informal and formal. Formal hedges have tightly clipped surfaces, normally down to ground level, so plants need a dense habit and must be tolerant of close clipping. Many conifers, for example, make excellent formal hedges.

Informal hedges are basically screens of shrubs or small trees. Here you can choose plants with colourful foliage, attractive flowers and/or autumn fruit.

Osmanthus delavayi. (Photo: Tim Sandall)

Griselinia littoralis 'Variegata'. *(Photo: Tim Sandall)*

Formal evergreen:
Buxus (box)
Chamaecyparis
Cupressus
× *Cupressocyparis leylandii* (Leyland's cypress)
Elaeagnus
Escallonia
Euonymus fortunei and *E. japonicus*
Griselinia
Ilex (holly)
Laurus nobilis (bay)
Ligustrum (privet)
Lonicera nitida
Osmanthus delavayi
Photinia
Prunus laurocerasus (laurel) and *P. lusitanica* (Portugal laurel)
Taxus (yew)
Thuja

Less formal evergreen:
Aucuba (spotted laurel)
Berberis

Brachyglottis (Dunedin Group) 'Sunshine'
Camellia
Choisya
Cotoneaster lacteus
Garrya elliptica
Myrtus
Nandina domestica
Olearia
Pieris
Pittosporum
Pyracantha
Rhododendron
Tamarix
Viburnum tinus

Cotoneaster conspicuus 'Decorus'. *(Photo: Tim Sandall)*

Formal deciduous:

Acer campestre
Carpinus betulus (hornbeam)
Fagus sylvatica (beech)

Informal deciduous:

Alnus (alder)
Crataegus (hawthorn)
Corylus (hazel)
Cotoneaster
Forsythia
Fuchsia
Hippophae
Potentilla
Prunux × *blireana, P. cerasifera, P. spinosa*
Ribes
Spiraea
Symphoricarpos

Rosmarinus officinalis 'Majorca Pink'.
(Photo: Tim Sandall)

Ilex × *altaclerensis* 'Lawsoniana'. *(Photo: Tim Sandall)*

Barrier:

Berberis
Chaenomeles
Ilex (holly)
Poncirus
Prunus spinosa
Pyracantha
Rosa
Ulex

Dwarf hedge/edge:

Buxus, dwarf cultivars

Lavandula
Podocarpus alpinus
Rosmarinus
Santolina
Sarcococca (winter box)
Rhododendron, dwarf cultivars

HEDGE SHAPING

When to prune, and the techniques used for informal hedges, are more or less the same as for a free-standing specimen (*see* the shrub section, page 30; and the tree section page 91). But any regular pruning should also consist of shaping the hedge outline, together with removing unwanted growth and trimming back to keep the hedge within bounds. It goes without saying that pruning flowering and fruiting hedges at the wrong time could result in no display the following year.

Plants used for less formal evergreen hedges only need adequate pruning to produce a solid but natural-looking outline. Formal hedges, however, will need regular and correct pruning to ensure they keep their shape and produce dense growth with a neat outline, with no bare areas or patches.

The aim with formal hedges is to create a tapered outline with the base wider than the top, producing a flat-topped or round-topped 'A'. The sides should slope inwards from the base so that light can reach the lower part of the hedge; if it has straight sides, or sides that taper inwards at the bottom, the lower part will be shaded and as a result will become bare or straggly. Hedges that are wider at the top are also prone to snow loading, when the upper, outer branches will be weighed down and will bend or even snap, causing the hedge to become untidy or damaged.

Dwarf hedges and edging don't need to be tapered and look better with vertical sides.

The easiest way to produce a flat-topped hedge is to cut to a straight edge or to use a garden line stretched between upright supports. To produce an even, round-topped hedge you may want to make a wooden or hardboard template cut to the required shape.

Once you have achieved the desired size and shape, all that is then needed is regular trimming, again using a straight edge or garden line. Most formal hedges are trimmed twice a year; deciduous hedges when they're dormant in winter and again in midsummer; and evergreens in late spring and late summer, although yew only needs cutting in the summer, and Leyland's cypress may need three cuts – a final cut during mid- to late August should deter excessive regrowth in autumn. Always check for nesting birds before starting the annual trim, and be sure that fledglings have flown.

OVERGROWN HEDGES

If not pruned regularly, or if left to its own devices, a hedge can soon get out of control. In such a situation, hard cutting back or renovation may be the answer to getting it back in shape.

Pruning laurel. (Photo: Tim Sandall)

Many hedges respond well to renovation pruning, for example beech, hawthorn, holly, hornbeam, *Lonicera nitida*, privet and yew. Conifer hedges, apart from yew, cannot be hard pruned, as they do not reshoot from old wood. Deciduous hedges are best renovated in mid-winter, evergreens in mid-spring. If possible, feed the hedge well the season prior to renovation, and feed and mulch the soil afterwards to aid recovery.

Hedges that respond well to hard pruning can be reduced by up to 50 per cent in height and width, but because hard pruning removes many growth buds, such severe treatment is best carried out in stages. If reducing both the height and width of the hedge, cut back the top and one side in the first year, and cut the other side the following year; if recovery is poor, delay the second cut for another twelve months. To ensure a dense, even surface you should cut back to at least 15–20cm (6–8in) *less* than the required final height and spread.

Conifers can be reduced in height in spring, though no more than one-third of the overall hedge height should be removed. As most conifers will not regrow from old wood, hard pruning should be avoided. If the hedge contains visible brown areas, tie in nearby green shoots to cover the patches. This can often be unsatisfactory, however, so individual plants may need to be replaced.

TOOLS

Hedges made from species with small leaves are best trimmed with shears or powered hedgetrimmers; those made from species with large leaves, such as laurel, should be cut using secateurs, loppers or saws. Using shears produces ragged, cut edges that look unsightly and often turn brown and die, detracting from the hedge's overall appearance. The individual shoots should be cut back to within the foliage canopy to hide the cut ends.

HIGH HEDGES

Recent legislation gives people whose gardens are overshadowed by tall hedges the opportunity to resolve the problem without involving lawyers. The Anti-Social Behaviour Act 2003, Part 8 gives people whose 'reasonable' enjoyment of their property is impaired by high hedges in close proximity the chance to alleviate the effects of overbearing living screens.

If high hedges affect you, contact your local council for guidance. The Communities and Local Government organization has produced a series of booklets detailing how to complain, and how to respond to complaints. These are available from the Communities and Local Government website: www.communities.gov.uk/index.asp?id=1127822.

A hedge, for the purposes of this law, is two or more trees in a line. Only evergreen hedges or semi-evergreen ones (that stay green most of the year) are covered; bamboo and ivy are not included.

The enforcement of hedge height reduction is limited to what is sufficient for those affected to enjoy reasonable use of their property, rather than to a specified height.

CHAPTER 9

Fruit and Nuts

Producing your own fruit at home or on an allotment is now, like vegetable growing, a very popular aspect of gardening. One of the major routes to success in growing just about any fruit – whether it's top (tree) fruit or soft fruit (cane, vine and bush) – is correct pruning. It is important to know what you're pruning and why, and this is quite straightforward providing you know what you're looking for. This chapter will help ensure success and regular, bumper crops.

POPULAR TREE FRUIT

The main tree fruits are apples, cherries, nectarines, peaches, pears and plums (including damsons and gages) – although other tree fruits are now becoming more popular (*see* page 127). They can be divided into two: those that produce stones (cherries, nectarines, peaches and plums), and those that produce pips (apples and pears). This affects when and, to some extent, how often you prune.

For example, stone fruit is susceptible to silver leaf and bacterial canker diseases, which tend to enter pruning cuts made in winter; as a result pruning must be delayed until after bud-burst in spring when training young trees, and until summer for established trees. Apples and pears are either pruned when dormant in winter (which encourages leafy growth) or in summer (which encourages flowering and fruiting growth).

OPPOSITE: Lemons are now popular home-grown fruit. (Photo: Tim Sandall)

Rootstocks

Most of the popular fruit trees are grafted on to a rootstock, and when buying it is essential to know which rootstock the cultivar is grafted on to. Rootstocks not only ensure the tree comes into regular cropping early in its life, but they also control the overall rate of growth and ultimate height of the tree, and some trained shapes are better on certain rootstocks.

Rootstocks are available to produce a wide range of ultimate heights, so instead of having a massive tree that takes over the garden, that must be constantly hacked back to keep it under control,

Cutting away dead fruits affected by disease. (Photo: Tim Sandall)

	Growth type	*Final height (approx.)*
Apple		
M27	Very dwarf	Up to 1.8m/6ft
M9	Dwarf	Up to 2.4–3m (8–10ft)
M26	Semi-dwarf	Up to 3–4.5m (10–15ft)
MM106	Semi-vigorous	Up to 3.5–5m (12–16ft)
MM111	Vigorous	Up to 4.5–6m (15–20ft)
Apricot		
St Julien A	Semi-vigorous	Up to 3.5–5m (12–16ft)
Cherry		
Tabel	Very dwarf	Up to 1.8m/6ft
Gisela 5	Dwarf	Up to 2.4–3m (8–10ft)
Damil	Semi-dwarf	Up to 3–4.5m (10–15ft)
Colt	Semi-vigorous	Up to 3.5–5m (12–16ft)
Inmil	Vigorous	Up to 4.5–6m (15–20ft)
Peach and nectarine		
Pixy	Dwarf	Up to 2.4–3m (8–10ft)
St Julien A	Semi-vigorous	Up to 3.5–5m (12–16ft)
Brompton	Vigorous	Up to 4.5–6m (15–20ft)
Pear		
Quince C	Dwarf	Up to 2.4–3m (8–10ft)
Quince A	Semi-vigorous	Up to 3.5–5m (12–16ft)
Plum, damson, gage		
Pixy	Dwarf	Up to 2.4–3m (8–10ft)
St Julien A	Semi-vigorous	Up to 3.5–5m (12–16ft)
Brompton	Vigorous	Up to 4.5–6m (15–20ft)
Myrobalan B	Vigorous	Up to 4.5–6m (15–20ft)

and for which you need stepladders or a cherry picker to get at the fruit, you can grow dwarf forms that you can pick at head height. Although the older, more vigorous rootstocks produce trees that need less pruning to crop regularly, some of the more modern ones produce smaller trees – though these may need more careful management.

The vigour of the fruiting cultivar will influence the overall final height of the tree.

Fruit Tree Shapes

Apart from rootstock and height, the other impor-tant decision to make is what 'shape' to grow. There is a wealth of forms and shapes that fruit trees can be trained and grown into, one of which will suit you, the fruit type and your particular needs. For instance, in small gardens dwarf bushes may be the best shape, or training espaliers or fans along a wall or fence. Dwarf bushes and cordons are particularly useful for fruit that isn't self-pollinating, and where you need to grow at least two different cultivars in order to get a good crop. In larger gardens where space isn't an issue – and you have a head for heights – you could grow full standards.

When choosing which shape to grow, remember the following:

- Some shapes are better for particular fruit.
- Some shapes are free-standing, others need permanent staking or the support of wires.
- Check the space available and the number of trees needed for pollination.
- Consider how much time and effort you are willing to give to the tree – some fruit and some shapes need a lot of care, attention and pruning.

Free-Standing Shapes

Bush

The bush fruit tree is the best size and shape for most average gardens – it doesn't grow too tall, and produces an excellent yield of fruit – especially where space for the reasonably spreading branches isn't an issue. The framework branches radiate outwards from a short main trunk, from 60–90cm (2–3ft) tall. The leader is pruned to produce a branched head with an open centre. Very dwarf bushes, such as apples grown on M27 rootstock, will need permanent staking.

This tree is suitable for apple, cherry, pear, plum, damson, gage, nectarine and peach.

Standard

Standards are grown with a clear trunk of anything up to 2m (6½ft). The crown is formed in the same way as for a bush, but the overall height and spread is much greater. Where space is more of an issue, half standards can be grown; these have a clear trunk of 1–1.2m (3¼–4ft).

It is suitable for apple, cherry, pear, plum, damson, gage, nectarine and peach.

Pyramid

The tree is short and compact, reaching no more than 2.4m (8ft) high. It tapers upwards, ensuring the lower branches receive plenty of sun to ripen the fruit.

The dwarf pyramid, grown to a maximum height of 2m (6½ft), is perfect for apples and pears.

It is mainly used for plum, gage and damson, but also apple, cherry and pear.

Spindle Bush

The spindle bush is popular in commercial orchards. It is basically a central-leader bush tree whose branches are trained horizontally to produce heavier crops. The branches are trained into a horizontal position from an early age, by tying them with string to pegs in the ground, or to the main trunk.

This bush is suitable for apple, pear, plum, damson and gage.

Columnar Trees

Ballerinas and minarettes are slender upright trees, almost like an upright cordon, that fruit on short spurs along the length of the main stem. Although often advertised as needing no pruning, they may need some in later years and can be treated as a cordon; *see* page 122.

Wire-supported Shapes

Fan

This is a decorative, heavy-cropping shape where a fan of branches originates from two low main arms on either side of a short main trunk. Horizontal supporting wires are spaced 30cm (1ft) apart.

It is suitable for most tree fruit, but especially stone fruit.

Espalier

In the espalier, pairs of opposite horizontal branches are trained off the main trunk. Horizontal supporting wires are spaced 45–60cm (18–24in) apart.

It is suitable for apples and pears.

Cordon

The cordon is the most compact shape – a single stem with fruiting spurs – perfect for apples and pears and some soft fruit (*see* page 133). Considering its size, an oblique cordon (grown at 45 degrees) is very productive: it produces excellent quality fruit, and several can be grown in a small space. Double (U), triple (W) and quadruple (double-U) upright espaliers are not only orna-mental, but produce good yields in a relatively small space.

Horizontal supporting wires are spaced 60cm, 90cm, 1.2m and 1.5m (2ft, 3ft, 4ft and 5ft) apart. The tree is actually tied to a supporting bamboo cane trained at the right angle.

It is suitable for apples and pears.

'V' and 'S' Modified Cordon Systems

These are comparatively new training methods, originally used in commercial orchards and which produce heavy crops.

In the 'V' system, two sets of 2m (6ft 6in) high posts are angled so that the top of each post is 1.2m (4ft) from the ground. Six cordons are planted between them 45cm (18in) apart, angled alternately one from the next.

In the 'S' system, the plants are trained up a 1.8m (6ft) high post, and in mid-summer the top of the stem is carefully bent back upon itself, and back in the opposite direction the following year to produce the 'S' shape.

The 'V' system is suitable for apples and pears, and the 'S' system for apples.

Stepover

The stepover is basically a single-tier espalier or cordon bent over at almost a right angle and trained horizontally to produce a very short trunk. This form is grown on an extremely dwarf-ing rootstock and can be used to edge a bed; they are something of a novelty rather than a good cropper.

It is suitable for apples.

Initial training of a bush fruit tree

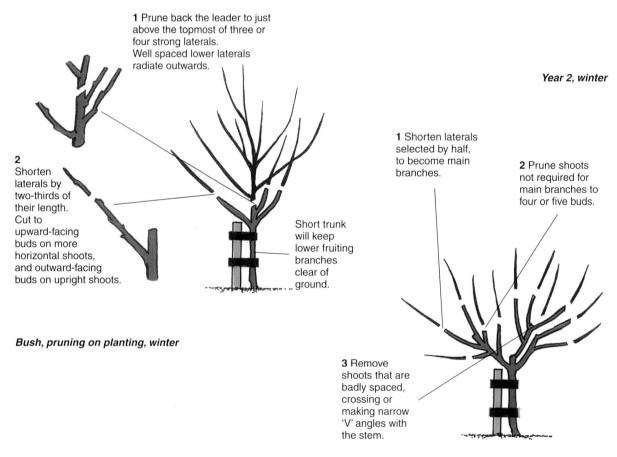

1 Prune back the leader to just above the topmost of three or four strong laterals. Well spaced lower laterals radiate outwards.

2 Shorten laterals by two-thirds of their length. Cut to upward-facing buds on more horizontal shoots, and outward-facing buds on upright shoots.

Short trunk will keep lower fruiting branches clear of ground.

Bush, pruning on planting, winter

Year 2, winter

1 Shorten laterals selected by half, to become main branches.

2 Prune shoots not required for main branches to four or five buds.

3 Remove shoots that are badly spaced, crossing or making narrow 'V' angles with the stem.

Year 3, winter (spur-bearers)

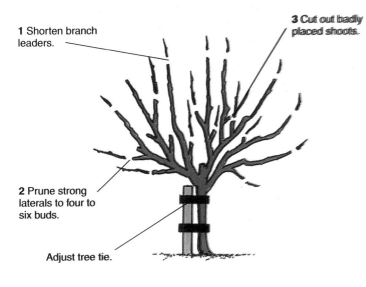

1 Shorten branch leaders.

3 Cut out badly placed shoots.

2 Prune strong laterals to four to six buds.

Adjust tree tie.

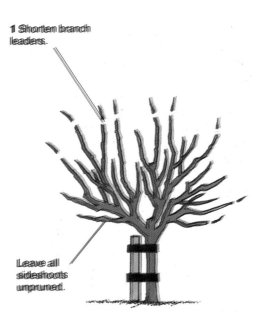

1 Shorten branch leaders.

Leave all sideshoots unpruned.

Family Trees

A family tree is a number of different cultivars (usually two or three) growing on a single root-stock. This is useful where space is at a premium and, providing the cultivars chosen are compatible with each other, ensures good pollination and fruit set. It is important to remember that the cultivars may differ in their vigour, and so pruning for each side of the tree may also differ. They are mainly grown as bushes and standards.

TRAINING TREE SHAPES

When growing tree fruit you have two options. Most people prefer to start with a relatively young tree already trained to the required shape; however, it is possible to do it from scratch yourself. The first option is the easiest for most gardeners; however, the second is more challenging and ultimately satisfying, and the plants are cheaper to buy – but you will have to wait a few years for the plant to reach cropping age.

If you are going to start from scratch, the first three or four years are the most crucial, and the tree will need annual attention to produce the required shape and woody framework on which the crop will be produced. You will need to buy a maiden tree – that is, a one-year-old tree that hasn't had any previous training.

Maidens are usually bought as bare-rooted trees and planted in the autumn or winter. You can choose from 'maiden whips', which have a single stem with no sideshoots, or from a 'feathered' maiden that has already produced young side-shoots, or feathers; the choice mainly depends on the type of shape you are training.

Bush, Half-standard, Standard and Pyramid

After planting a maiden tree, shorten the main stem to around 70cm (28in), cutting just above a bud. By the following winter, the tree should have produced strong primary branches. Select four or five of the strongest that are coming out wide from the trunk, and cut them back by about half to an outward-facing bud. Remove all other branches where they join the main stem (*see* illustration on page 118).

During the following year the tree will produce secondary branches. In the winter these should be cut back by about half, again to an outward-facing bud. The laterals on these are cut back to four or five buds to help induce the fruiting spurs (*see* illustration on page 119).

This basic pruning is the same for half-standards, standards and pyramids.

Espaliers

Plant an unfeathered maiden tree, then cut back the main stem to 5–7.5cm (2–3in) above the first supporting wire.

The uppermost bud will then shoot to become the new leader; this is tied to a vertical cane tied to

Initial training of an espalier

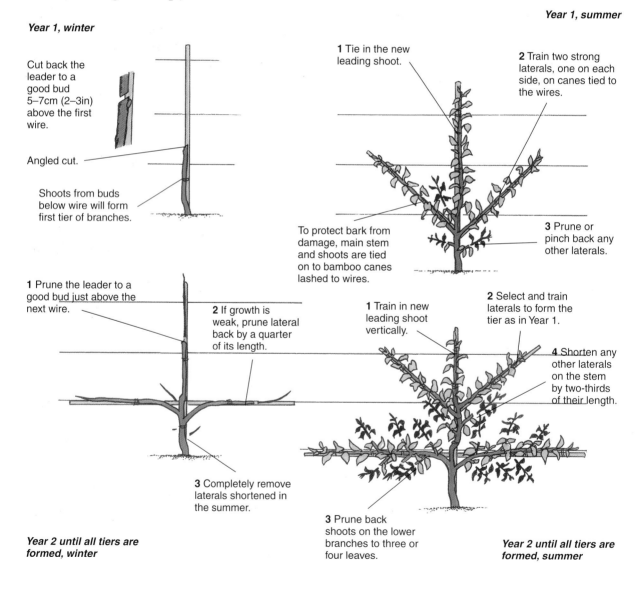

Year 1, winter

Cut back the leader to a good bud 5–7cm (2–3in) above the first wire.

Angled cut.

Shoots from buds below wire will form first tier of branches.

Year 1, summer

1 Tie in the new leading shoot.

2 Train two strong laterals, one on each side, on canes tied to the wires.

3 Prune or pinch back any other laterals.

To protect bark from damage, main stem and shoots are tied on to bamboo canes lashed to wires.

1 Prune the leader to a good bud just above the next wire.

2 If growth is weak, prune lateral back by a quarter of its length.

3 Completely remove laterals shortened in the summer.

Year 2 until all tiers are formed, winter

1 Train in new leading shoot vertically.

2 Select and train laterals to form the tier as in Year 1.

4 Shorten any other laterals on the stem by two-thirds of their length.

3 Prune back shoots on the lower branches to three or four leaves.

Year 2 until all tiers are formed, summer

the supporting wires. The next two buds will shoot to become the first tier of horizontal branches. These should be allowed to grow out from the main stem, and tied to bamboo canes tied to the supporting wires as they grow. In late summer/ early autumn untie these two stems from the wires, carefully lower them to the first supporting wire, and tie them in horizontally.

In winter, cut back the main stem to just above the second supporting wire – preferably to a bud on the opposite side to the cut made in the first winter. If one of the horizontal shoots is weaker than the other, cut it back by about a quarter.

The next three buds on the main stem will shoot and should be treated in exactly the same way as in the first year.

Fans

Plant a young, feathered tree with two low, strong

laterals – preferably 25–30cm (10–12in) from the ground. Tie these to 1.8m (6ft) long bamboo canes tied at an angle of 45 degrees to the supporting wires. Shorten the laterals to 40–45cm (16–18in) from the main leader, cutting to a downward-facing bud. Then cut back the main leader to just above the topmost lateral. Cut back any remaining laterals on the leader to two buds.

During the following summer, tie in the two main laterals as they grow – these will form the main arms of the fan. Also tie in any sideshoots off the main laterals as they develop, especially those lower down on each arm, to ensure they fill in the area being covered. The aim is for even spacing and development on both arms. Pinch out or cut back any sideshoots that aren't needed.

Establish the main framework during the next two years by shortening sideshoots in spring to leave 60–75cm (24–30in) of the previous year's growth.

Initial training of a fan

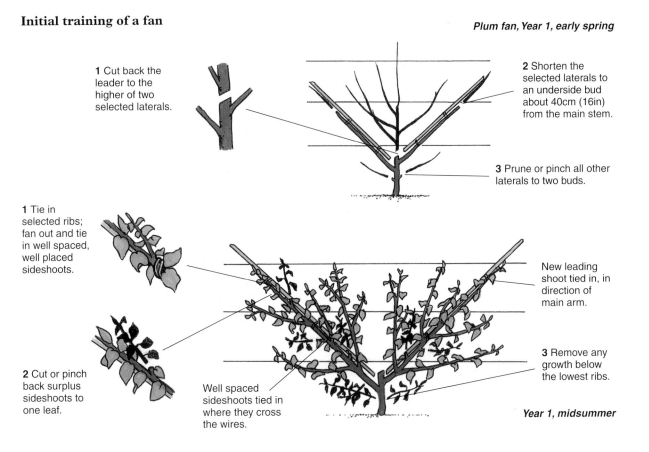

Plum fan, Year 1, early spring

1 Cut back the leader to the higher of two selected laterals.

2 Shorten the selected laterals to an underside bud about 40cm (16in) from the main stem.

3 Prune or pinch all other laterals to two buds.

1 Tie in selected ribs; fan out and tie in well spaced, well placed sideshoots.

2 Cut or pinch back surplus sideshoots to one leaf.

Well spaced sideshoots tied in where they cross the wires.

New leading shoot tied in, in direction of main arm.

3 Remove any growth below the lowest ribs.

Year 1, midsummer

Initial training of a cordon

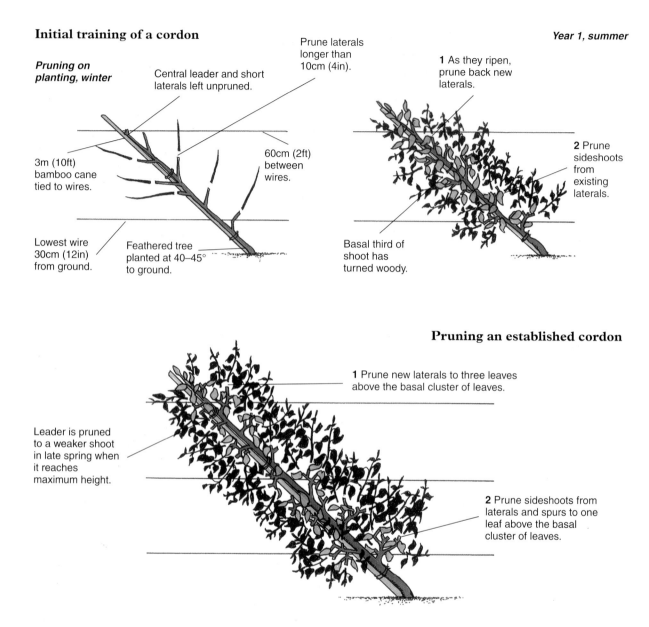

Year 1, summer

Pruning on planting, winter

Central leader and short laterals left unpruned.

Prune laterals longer than 10cm (4in).

3m (10ft) bamboo cane tied to wires.

60cm (2ft) between wires.

Lowest wire 30cm (12in) from ground.

Feathered tree planted at 40–45° to ground.

1 As they ripen, prune back new laterals.

2 Prune sideshoots from existing laterals.

Basal third of shoot has turned woody.

Pruning an established cordon

1 Prune new laterals to three leaves above the basal cluster of leaves.

Leader is pruned to a weaker shoot in late spring when it reaches maximum height.

2 Prune sideshoots from laterals and spurs to one leaf above the basal cluster of leaves.

Cordons

Plant a feathered maiden or two-year-old tree with well spaced sideshoots at an angle of 45 degrees, tying it to a bamboo cane tied in at the same angle to the supporting wires. Do not prune the leader or short laterals, but those 10cm (4in) or longer are cut back to three or four buds.

In the first summer, as new laterals on the main stem ripen, prune them back to three leaves above the basal cluster of leaves, and sideshoots on existing laterals to one leaf to start forming the fruiting spurs.

PRUNING ESTABLISHED TREES

Always remember the principles of 'Why prune?' detailed in Chapter 1 on page 5. This should be your first reason for getting out the secateurs, as well as pruning to build up fruiting wood.

Also remember the pruning techniques described in Chapter 2 on page 15, making the correct types of cut, and curing the post-pruning depression (*see* page 20).

Pruning too much, too often or too hard can result in an excess of young growth (water shoots) that can take several years to reach fruiting size and so affect the overall yield of the tree.

Apple

Most free-standing apples are pruned in winter when dormant, while wire-trained forms and dwarf pyramids are pruned in summer to help restrict growth and encourage fruiting.

Apple cultivars can be divided into whether they are spur bearers or tip bearers, and this influences how they are pruned. Tip bearers are also best avoided when growing as wire-supported forms due to their pruning requirements.

Pruning an established apple bush

Spur pruning (for spur bearers) in winter

1 Shorten weak branch leaders by half, strong ones by a quarter.

2 Prune other new shoots to four to six buds.

Well placed, strong shoot will be eventual replacement when low branch is pulled down by weight of fruit.

3 As the bush matures, shorten or remove any overcrowded spurs.

Some shorter, well placed shoots may be left unpruned.

2 Tip-prune branch leaders or they will be bowed down by fruits that develop at the tip.

Replacement growth resulting from pruning in previous winter.

1 Cut back a proportion of older fruited wood to a young shoot or basal bud.

Larger, old branch removed to reduce overcrowding in bush centre.

Longer stem length between shoots is typical of tip-bearers.

Renewal pruning (for tip-bearers) in winter

Pruning an established plum fan

Summer

1 Tie laterals using soft twine tied in figures of eight.

2 When they have nine to twelve leaves, cut or pinch back laterals not required, later pinching out any regrowth.

3 Cut out any worn-out wood, and any badly placed, unhealthy, or excessively strong and upright new shoots.

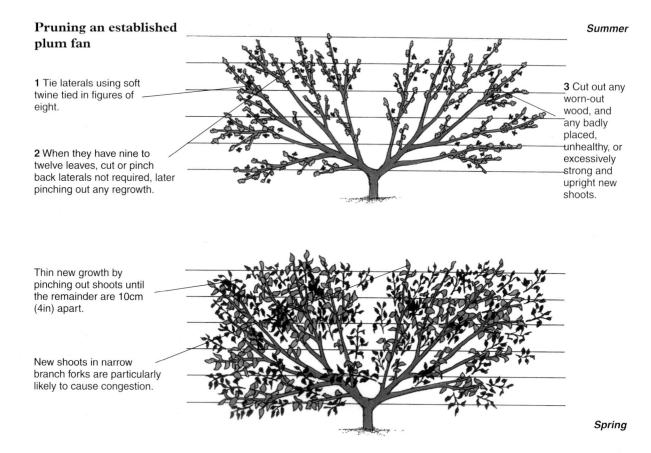

Thin new growth by pinching out shoots until the remainder are 10cm (4in) apart.

New shoots in narrow branch forks are particularly likely to cause congestion.

Spring

Most apples are spur bearers, producing fruit on short fruit-producing sideshoots, or spurs, that are three years old or older along the branches. Tip bearers produce their fruit at or near the tips of shoots made the previous year. Popular examples include 'Bramley's Seedling', 'Blenheim Orange', 'Discovery', 'Epicure', 'Lord Lambourne' and 'Worcester Pearmain'.

Free-standing apple trees are pruned to remove surplus wood and to encourage a steady supply of new shoots that bear fruit in later years. Left unpruned, growth becomes congested, with older branches bearing fewer flowers and poor quality fruit. Keep the centre of the tree open by removing larger branches; if several larger branches need removing, then spread the work over two or three winters.

Once the basic framework has been achieved, the remaining pruning depends on whether the tree is a spur or tip bearer. For spur bearers, shorten each branch leader by about one-third of the previous year's growth to a bud facing in the required direction. Cut back young laterals growing from the permanent branches to five or six buds. Shorter, well placed shoots can be left unpruned. On older trees you may need to thin out some of the spur systems as they become overcrowded, by cutting out some of the older, more complicated spurs from each system.

For tip bearers, tip prune the leaders of each main branch and the most vigorous laterals to encourage more tip-bearing shoots the following summer by just pruning back to the first strong bud. Leave unpruned any laterals that are less than about 30cm (12in) long. Cut back a proportion of older fruited wood to a young shoot or leaf bud to reduce congestion.

Established apple cordons, dwarf pyramids, espaliers and stepovers should be pruned in summer when the basal third of new shoots have

Pruning an established sweet cherry fan

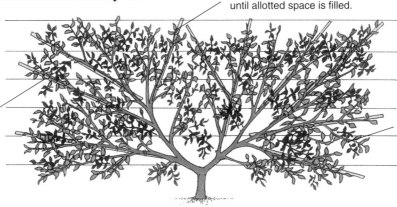

Early summer

Leave branch leaders unpruned until allotted space is filled.

1 Tie in some new shoots where they can fill spaces in the framework. String tied vertically between wires provides more attachment points.

2 Shorten all other new shoots: once they have eight to twelve leaves, pinch or cut them back to six or seven leaves, pinching any subsequent growth to one leaf.

Acid cherry fan

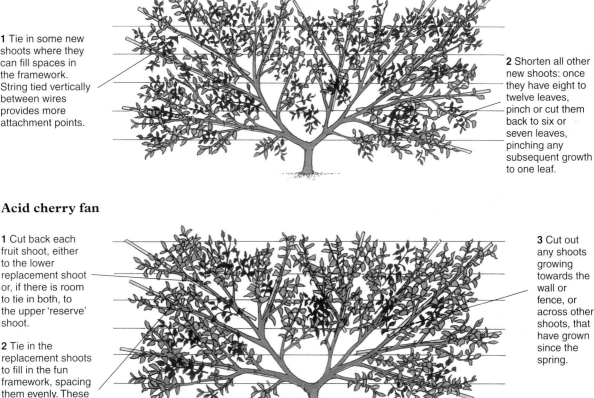

1 Cut back each fruit shoot, either to the lower replacement shoot or, if there is room to tie in both, to the upper 'reserve' shoot.

2 Tie in the replacement shoots to fill in the fun framework, spacing them evenly. These shoots should fruit next year.

3 Cut out any shoots growing towards the wall or fence, or across other shoots, that have grown since the spring.

Pruning after fruiting

turned woody. The sideshoots that come off the main stem, and which are at least 23cm (9in) long, are shortened to the third leaf above the basal cluster of leaves. Sideshoots from existing laterals or spurs are cut back to the first leaf beyond the basal cluster of leaves. Shoots shorter than 23cm (9in) long are left unpruned. However, in warm climates sideshoots that are 15–23cm (6–9in) long can be pruned. If secondary growth is produced, cut it back to one bud in autumn. Remove completely any over-vigorous, upright shoots.

Renovation of tall and overcrowded trees is best staged over several years as hard pruning results in strong new growth at the expense of cropping. As well as removing unwanted and unnecessary growth, thin out spur systems that are over-congested and remove weaker shoots where possible. This should result in larger and better quality fruit. Heavy pruning may result in water shoots growing the following summer. From these, select potential replacement branches; the final shoot spacing should ideally be at least 30cm (1ft) apart, so remove all other badly placed growth, and thin, overcrowded shoots.

Apricot

Apricots produce their flowers early in the year, and as a result can be subject to frost damage. In warmer regions, and when using the latest hardier cultivars, it is possible to grow them in a bush tree shape. In cooler regions it is better to grow them as fans trained against a south-facing wall.

Fruit is produced on growth that is at least two years old and at the base of one-year-old shoots. Being a stone fruit, they should never be pruned in winter: when training young plants they can be pruned in spring, and established trees should be pruned in summer. Dying back of the shoot tips is quite common, and affected shoots should be cut back to a healthy bud.

After planting, tip back the leader to encourage the development of sideshoots.

Established bush trees are pruned in the same way as plums: *see* page 127 for details; fans are pruned as for plum fans, *see* page 124.

Cherry

Being a stone fruit, cherries must be pruned in summer. There are two main types of cherry: the sweet or dessert cherries, and the acid or sour cherries – but there are also duke cherries, which are a hybrid between the two. Acid cherries are pruned differently to sweet and duke cherries.

Sweet cherries produce fruit at the base of the previous year's growth and on older wood. Keep the pruning of free-standing trees to a minimum, although overcrowded branches may need removing. With fans, start by rubbing away unwanted buds, especially those growing towards or away from the wall. In mid-summer cut back the sideshoots to five or six leaves from the base, and then shorten these again after fruiting or in early autumn, to three or four leaves.

Acid cherries fruit on shoots produced the previous year. On free-standing trees aim to cut out some of the wood that has fruited each year as well as old, congested growth to produce space for existing young growth and produce new shoots. For fans, as fruit only develops on young shoots, each year after harvest cut back each fruited stem to the replacement shoot at its base. Also rub out inward- or outward-facing buds in spring.

Peach and Nectarine

As peaches and nectarines are stone fruit they must be pruned in summer.

Peaches and nectarines fruit on shoots produced the previous year. On free-standing trees, aim to cut out some of the wood that has fruited each year, as well as old, congested growth, to produce space for existing young growth and also new shoots.

On fans, rub out inward- or outward-facing buds in spring. Then on each flowering shoot, select one good lateral at the base (this will replace the flowering/fruiting stem the following year) and one higher up (this is insurance in case the lower one fails). In late spring cut back the flowering shoot and both laterals to six leaves. After fruiting, cut out the flowering/fruiting stem (unless it is needed to fill a gap in the fan), and tie in its replacement.

When pruning to produce a new shoot, always cut to a pointed growth bud rather than the plump fruit bud.

Fruit will need to be thinned out. Start by thinning to one or two fruits per fruiting cluster, and if necessary, thin again when the fruit is a little larger to leave each fruit 15–23cm (6–9in) apart, the closer distance for nectarines and wall-trained peaches.

A good crop of pears. (Photo: Tim Sandall)

Pear

Pears grow in a similar way to apples and are treated in the same way. They do, however, tend to have a more upright growth habit and produce fruiting spur systems more easily; these can become very congested if not thinned out in later years.

There are very few tip-bearing cultivars, most are spur bearers.

Established pear cordons, dwarf pyramids and espaliers are usually ready for pruning a week or two earlier than apples.

Plum, Gage and Damson

Summer is the time to prune plums to avoid disease infection.

Plums fruit at the base of one-year-old shoots as well as along the length of older shoots. This means that the young growth does not need regular pruning, since the newest stems bear a good crop. Pruning of most free-standing plum trees should be kept to a minimum, although overcrowded branches may need removing.

When pruning an established fan-trained plum, remove some of the older wood if there is a strong young shoot lower down to fill in the gap. To help keep its shape, cut back all new sideshoots to six leaves, with regrowth pinched out at one leaf. After fruiting, shorten these pruned shoots again to one to three leaves; this allows the tree to direct its energies into next year's fruit buds.

For plums that are grown as pyramids, shorten new shoots on main stems to about 20cm (8in) and strong sideshoots to 15cm (6in).

Plums can produce a lot of fruit, which can cause the branches to bend and snap, and thinning is often needed; aim to thin to 7.5–10cm (3–4in) apart.

Pruning old, neglected plum trees should be staged over several years as they respond to larger pruning cuts by sending up a mass of new shoots, which should be thinned to leave just one or two.

FRUIT THINNING

Some fruit trees produce large clusters of many fruitlets. If all the fruit is allowed to develop they will be small with a poor flavour. The weight may also break the branches. In such cases it is a good idea to thin out the crop to ensure the remaining fruit grow to a decent size and receive plenty of light so they ripen and produce a good flavour.

OTHER TREE FRUIT

Citrus

There are numerous different types of citrus fruit, lime, lemon, orange and grapefruit being the most commonly grown. They are not frost hardy and need winter protection in cool climates. Although it is possible to grow them from pips, the resulting plants take several years to reach fruiting age, and the fruit is usually poor or insipid. It is far better to buy and grow a named cultivar that has been grafted on to a rootstock.

Pruning of established plants is best kept to a minimum. Although most citrus in warm climates can be pruned at nearly any time of year, in cooler climates it is best to prune young trees in spring or summer; the best time is immediately after pruning. Established trees can be pruned during or after harvesting.

Start by removing congested growth in spring, especially that growing into the middle of the plant, and for bushy growth, pinch out the shoot tips in summer. When harvesting, cut back the fruited shoot to the next young shoot, as it will not fruit again.

If renovation is needed, prune back the oldest shoots by two-thirds in early spring.

BIENNIAL BEARING

Some fruit trees, but especially apples and pears, can experience biennial bearing – that is, they only produce a crop, whether reasonable or any at all, every other year. There are numerous factors that affect this, and some cultivars are more prone than others, but one of the main reasons is that in an 'on' year the tree produces more fruit than it can cope with. It is, however, possible to help overcome biennial bearing, and prevent the tree having an 'off' year.

In the winter following an 'off' year, prune as normal but leave unpruned as many one-year-old shoots as possible. These will not produce fruit the next year, but will produce fruit buds for the following year – that is, the next 'off' year.

Another cure is to thin the blossom, removing nine out of every ten blossom trusses within a week of flowering.

Fig tree in fruit. (Photo: Tim Sandall)

Figs

Figs prefer a warm climate, with long, hot summers in order to produce a good crop of fruit. In warm areas they can be grown as a free-standing bush or a half-standard tree, with a main trunk between 60–120cm (2–4ft) high. In cooler climates they are best grown as fans against a warm, south-facing wall, or they can be grown as dwarf bushes, with a stem length of 40cm (16in), in containers that are moved to a frost-free place for the winter.

Figs like to have their roots restricted, so planting in a container is often a good idea. Otherwise, free-standing or wall-trained plants should be planted in a 60cm (2ft) square pit lined with paving slabs or similar; or they should be root pruned every couple of years – *see* page 19.

They have an unusual fruiting pattern, in that fruit at three stages of development may be present at the same time. First to ripen are the young embryo fruit that overwintered from the previous year; second are those that form in the spring on the new growth; and simultaneously, embryo fruit for the following year forms near the tips of new shoots. In warm climates, this results in a long fruiting season, though in cooler climates the summer conditions are usually not good enough for fruit to ripen in one year.

As a result, the only fruit that ripens and is edible is that which overwintered as embryo fruit. In such conditions, pruning aims to encourage embryo fig formation, and to provide optimum conditions for these to ripen the following year. Only embryo fruit that forms towards the end of the growing season should be kept; those fruits appearing earlier should be removed as they will be too big to withstand cold winter weather.

The main pruning is carried out in spring, once any danger of severe frost has passed. In cooler climates all new shoots should also be cut back to five or six leaves in summer.

Pruning a fig tree. (Photo: Geoff Hodge)

For fig trees and bushes, spring pruning involves removing damaged shoots and those that are badly placed or overcrowded, to encourage an open, spreading habit. Leggy shoots and old branches can be cut back to 5–7.5cm (2–3in) to encourage new growth. In summer, pinch out any new shoots at five or six leaves to encourage fruit formation

To produce a fan fig, develop the branch structure as recommended for any other fan; *see* page 121. Aim for five or six main ribs on each side, tying in sideshoots to fill in the framework. Once the framework has been formed you can start summer pruning. Once established, prune in spring to remove some old wood, and cut back a few young shoots to one bud as well as pruning in summer.

Loquat (Eriobotrya japonica)

The loquat needs a warm summer to fruit; cold winters may reduce flowering. Flowers and fruit are formed on the current year's growth from about five years after planting.

Plants are trained as a multi-stemmed tree on a short trunk. Newly planted trees should have branches shortened by one-third as plants come into growth in spring to encourage branching.

Established trees need no regular pruning, although excess sideshoots should be thinned out.

Medlar (Mespilus germanica)

Medlar fruit need to be fully ripened on the tree, then picked and stored in a cool, dark place until the flesh starts to 'rot' and turn soft, a process known as 'bletting'; they are then made into preserves. The tree itself also has distinctive flowers and attractive autumn colours.

The fruit is borne on naturally occurring short spurs formed on older wood.

Train as a branch-headed standard with strong, well spaced branches. Little pruning is needed after the branch framework has established. Some old, fruited wood can be removed in winter if needed. Medlars do not respond well to hard pruning and renovation.

Mulberry (Morus nigra *and* M. rubra)

The black mulberry, *Morus nigra*, *M. rubra* and their cultivars are the best ones to grow for quality edible fruit.

Help maintain the central leader for as long as possible, or train in a replacement if it fails. As the tree matures, the uppermost sideshoots will naturally overtake the leader to form a broad-headed tree. Pruning is best kept to a minimum as too much pruning, especially renovation pruning, can lead to excessive water shoot production; these affect subsequent growth and need thinning out. Any pruning should be carried out in winter when the tree is fully dormant to prevent sap bleeding.

For pruning *Morus alba*, the white mulberry, *see* page 98.

Pruning an olive tree. (Photo: Tim Sandall)

Olive

Olives are slow-growing evergreens that need a cool winter to crop well, although they won't tolerate temperatures below −10°C (14°F).

Trees normally start to fruit after five years, and can fruit for many years. The fruit are formed on the previous year's growth. Prune in early to mid-spring.

On young trees, select four well spaced sideshoots at a height of 90cm–1.2m (3–4ft) to form the crown; then let the head form naturally. Old and unproductive wood can be removed to promote new growth that will flower the following year. Thin out overcrowded shoots in the middle of the crown.

Olives can also be grown fan trained on a wall, by tying in growth to form a fan framework. Prune out outward-growing and badly placed shoots.

Olives respond well to hard pruning and can be renovated by pruning down to ground level.

Quince (Cydonia oblonga)

Quinces are best grown as a bush form. To start a quince from scratch, follow the instructions for training and pruning a bush tree on page 118. Once established, the tree may become crowded in the middle, and vigorous shoots and those that are not needed or are causing congestion, should be removed in winter to keep the centre of the tree open. But never prune too hard, or vigorous re-growth will be produced.

NUTS

Growing your own nuts at home is on the increase. Old favourites such as cobnuts, filberts and walnuts are being joined by the more exotic almond, macadamia and sweet chestnut, all three of which need long, warm summers to fruit well.

Growing is fairly straightforward: almonds are grown like peaches; macadamia nut, sweet chest-nut and walnut are grown as central-leader stan-dards (*see* page 87 for details); and cobnuts and filberts can be grown in a variety of ways.

Almond

Although hardy, almonds need a warm summer to crop well. Although they can be grown as free-standing trees, they may be better trained as a fan in cooler climates. Being a member of the *Prunus* family, pruning should be carried out in summer and is best kept to a minimum.

Both trees and fans are produced and main-tained in the same way as peaches; *see* page 126 for details.

Cobnuts and Filberts

Cobnuts and filberts usually crop well in most climates, especially if a named cultivar is chosen. Although they can grow fairly large, training and regular pruning produces a more compact habit and improves cropping.

They can be grown as multi-stemmed bushes, with one or two of the oldest stems removed at ground level in late winter, or they can be cop-piced. However, for best results they are grown as an open-centred bush on a 40–45cm (16–18in) leg.

To train a young tree, start with a plant with three or four laterals at this height. Cut back the leader to the topmost of these, and shorten these laterals to 23–25cm (9–10in); remove any other laterals.

During the next two years allow ten to twelve shoots to develop to form the main branches, and remove any growth below the main branches in winter.

In late summer, snap or partially break any long, vigorous shoots at half their length (a process known as brutting). In winter, prune back the brutted shoots to three to five buds.

As plants get older you will need to remove one or two old and worn-out branches so that these can be replaced by new growth.

For pruning ornamental hazels, *see* page 37.

Macadamia Nut

The macadamia nut is becoming more popular, although trees will only tolerate light frosts and need a long, hot growing season to fruit well.

Train them as a central-leader tree with a clear trunk of about 1m (3ft) and well spaced, spreading branches. Young trees tend to produce shoots in whorls of three. If these develop, select one to produce the main branch and cut back the other two to 1–2cm (½–¾in); the shoots from the buds on these short stubs develop into the flowering shoots.

Established trees need little or no pruning.

Sweet Chestnut

When growing the sweet chestnut for its nuts, always choose a cultivar that is a reliable cropper, such as 'Marron de Lyon'.

Train it as a central-leader standard with evenly, well spaced, wide V-angled sideshoots coming from the main stem. Established trees need little in the way of pruning, although it is a good idea to reduce the spread of mature branches by shortening them. Pruning should be carried out when the tree is dormant, in autumn and winter, although minor pruning can be done in late summer.

For pruning ornamental sweet chestnuts, *see* page 93.

Walnut

The walnuts grown for fruiting are mainly

cultivars of *Juglans regia*, including 'Broadview', 'Buccaneer' and 'Franquette'.

They can be grown either as a central-leader standard, or kept smaller by removing the leader. Central-leader standards should have their lowest branches cut back to the trunk while still young. To keep both forms relatively compact and bushy, the new growth of the side branches can be pinched out at the fifth or sixth leaf during summer. Otherwise, where space is not limited, the tree can be allowed to grow unhindered, with pruning kept to a minimum.

Established walnuts are best left unpruned. Where pruning is necessary it is important to do it between mid-summer and early autumn; pruning from winter to mid-spring will lead to bleeding from the cuts.

Walnuts do not tolerate hard pruning.

For pruning ornamental walnuts, *see* page 97.

SOFT FRUIT

Soft fruit is much easier to look after than tree fruit, and even with little or no pruning will produce a reasonable crop. The skill is to keep the plants strong and healthy so that they give the biggest crops for as long as possible; most soft fruit can crop prolifically for many years if well looked after. Feeding and good husbandry will help, but correct pruning is the true key to success.

Soft fruit can be grown and, in some cases, trained to take up very little space, so every garden should be able to accommodate at least a few well grown bushes. And home-grown fruit tastes better and is fresher than anything you can buy.

Soft fruit can be divided into three basic types: cane fruit (raspberries, blackberries and the numerous so-called hybrid berries); bush fruit (currants, gooseberries and blueberries); and vine fruit (grapes, kiwi fruit, passion fruit). Nor should we forget the strawberry, a herbaceous, non-woody plant that doesn't need pruning – apart from cutting off old or diseased leaves.

Many soft fruit types produce spines or rough, hairy bristles that will attack the unsuspecting gardener – so it pays to wear strong gloves and suitable clothing when dealing with them.

Cane Fruit

These produce annual sturdy canes from ground level. They start to fruit in the second year after planting.

Raspberries
There are two basic types: the common summer-fruiting type, which produces fruit on the previous year's growth; and the increasingly popular autumn-fruiting type that fruits on the current year's growth. This difference affects how the two types are pruned once established.

Both summer- and autumn-fruiting raspberries are trained and tied in to three tensioned horizontal wires fixed at 75cm (2½ft), 1.05m (3½ft) and 1.65m (5½ft) from soil level; these wires are firmly anchored on sturdy posts positioned at the row ends.

After planting the canes, usually in autumn or winter, cut them back to 25–30cm (9–12in) from ground level. New canes will grow from the ground during the summer, and will start cropping the following year. Cut out and remove very weak canes and tie in all others to the three horizontal wires as they grow; the new canes should be spaced about 10cm (4in) apart. In subsequent years, pruning differs for the two types.

For summer-fruiting raspberries: after cropping, completely cut out the fruited canes. Tie in up to eight of the best new replacement canes per plant spaced 7.5–10cm (3–4in) apart. In late winter, tip back the canes to 15cm (6in) above the top training wire.

For autumn-fruiting raspberries: prune all canes to ground level in late winter, before new growth starts. Tie in up to eight of the best new replacement canes per plant, spaced 7.5–10cm (3–4in) apart. You can, if you wish, leave one or two canes intact and these will produce earlier fruit. Do not remove the fruited canes after cropping.

Blackberries and Hybrid Berries
Blackberries and hybrid berries are very vigorous growers, and strict training and pruning will ensure that plants are kept manageable and within bounds. Training will also help the fruit ripen and

make it easier to pick, by keeping the fruiting canes and the new canes separate.

There are numerous hybrid berries such as boysenberry, loganberry, silvanberry, sunberry, tayberry, tummelberry, veitchberry, and wineberry (*Rubus phoenicolasius*). Some are crosses between recognized fruit (for instance, the tayberry is a cross between a blackberry and a raspberry), others have a more mixed parentage.

They are all pruned and trained in the same way. Pruning consists of cutting out fruited canes at ground level once harvest is complete, then tying in the new canes in their place. If too few new canes are produced, keep some of the old ones (although these will be less fruitful after their first year of cropping). Tie in young growth. In spring, any frost-damaged growth can be removed.

A sturdy support is needed, so train plants on a system of four taut horizontal wires, supported by sturdy posts, 30cm (12in) apart, the lowest 90cm (3ft) from soil level, the highest 1.8m (6ft). Weaker-growing types, such as the thornless loganberries, can also be trained around a single upright post.

Four training systems are generally used: fan, alternate, rope and weaving.

Fan: A compact system for less vigorous types. The fruiting canes are spread out on the supporting wires, and the new canes are tied together vertically in the middle of the plant. These are lowered and tied into position once the fruiting canes have been cut out.

Alternate: The fruiting canes are grown in one direction from the plant, and the new canes are tied in, in the opposite direction as they grow.

Rope: Fruiting canes are twisted together and tied, evenly spaced along the lower wires. The non-fruiting canes are either tied on to the top wire, or supported using bamboo canes. When the fruited canes are cut out, the new ones are divided among the lower wires.

Weaving: This is a good space-saving method for very vigorous types, though it takes more time than the other methods. Fruiting canes are trained in a serpentine manner on the lower wires, the new ones up the middle and along the top wire. When the fruited canes are removed, the new ones are lowered and woven in place.

Bush Fruit

As their name suggests, plants fruit on sturdy, long-lived bushes. Pruning is aimed at producing a more or less permanent framework of branches. These may come from a single stem or leg (red- and whitecurrants and gooseberries), or they may be multi-stemmed (blackcurrants and blueberries).

Gooseberries

Gooseberries are trained to form an open-centred bush, 1.2–1.8m (4–6ft) high, on a short stem or leg, with a strong framework of eight to twelve main branches arising from the stem. They produce their fruit on spurs on older wood and at the base of the previous year's growth.

After planting, shorten all the shoots by half to three-quarters to an outward-facing bud; simply tip them back to a healthy bud if the nursery has already carried this out. If the cultivar has a more open, pendant habit, prune to an upward-facing bud. Sideshoots will then form, from which eight to twelve are selected to form the main branches.

In the following winter, cut back the main branches by half to three-quarters. Then in the next winter shorten these by about a quarter. Shorten the remaining shoots to four or five buds.

In future years, in mid-summer prune by shortening the current season's growth to five leaves, except those that are needed to extend the height or form branches. In winter, spur-prune the same shoots, reducing them to one to three buds from their base, and shorten branch leaders by a quarter to a suitably positioned bud, aiming to keep the centre of the bush open. Remove any shoots developing on the leg.

Red- and Whitecurrants

The pruning is similar to gooseberries, the aim being to form an open-centred bush on a short stem with eight to ten main branches. They produce fruit at the base of sideshoots formed the

A redcurrant bush before (left) and after (right) pruning. (Photo: Geoff Hodge)

previous year. These are pruned in winter to produce short fruiting spurs that fruit annually.

After planting, cut back each main shoot by half to an outward-facing bud, or an upward-facing one on a pendant stem, and remove any weak growth.

In the following winter, shorten these main shoots by half, and select up to a further six strong shoots to form the other main branches: cut these back by half. Badly placed shoots and weak sideshoots are cut back to one bud to encourage strong growth.

In subsequent years, cut back that year's growth in winter so that the bush has its main branches covered with short fruiting spurs. This means cutting back all shoots from the main branches to one bud. Very old, unproductive and unhealthy growth can be removed by cutting it back to a strong, vigorous shoot.

In mid-summer you can shorten the current season's growth to five leaves, except those shoots that are needed to extend or form branches; however, this isn't essential.

Old, neglected gooseberries and red- and whitecurrants can be renovated by removing all the dead, damaged and dying growth, also the weak, crossing and rubbing branches, together with the unwanted main branches, and then cutting back the sideshoots to one or two buds. However, if the plant is very old it may be better to replace it.

Where space is an issue, gooseberries and red- and whitecurrants can be grown as restricted shapes, such as cordons, fans and standards, providing ornamental fruiting garden features.

Cordons: These are grown on taught, free-standing, horizontal training wires or those attached to walls; the wires should be spaced 30cm (12in) apart.

Plant a single-stemmed young plant, and in the first spring after planting, cut back the main stem by half, and all other shoots to one bud. In early summer tie in the main stem and prune back the new sideshoots to five leaves. In the following winter prune back the sideshoots to one or two buds. Shorten the main stem by one-third of the new growth; this is done every winter until the cordon has reached the required height.

When the plant is mature, the main stem should be stopped at five leaves in early summer, and the sideshoots pruned back to one or two buds of the old growth in winter.

Fans: These should be trained against walls or fences on taught, horizontal wires 30cm (12in) apart. Plant a single-stemmed young plant and, after planting, cut back the stem to two strong sideshoots or buds about 15cm (6in) from the ground that can be trained in opposite directions to form the main fan arms. As these sideshoots grow, tie them to bamboo canes tied to the wires at an angle of 45 degrees. In the following winter, cut back both shoots by half and remove all other shoots.

During the summer, select three or four sideshoots on each of the two main arms to train as the main ribs of the fan. Remove vigorous surplus shoots, but retain any weaker ones, but shorten them to three or four leaves. In the following winter, cut back the shoots forming the ribs by half, and their sideshoots back to one bud. In summer, shorten all sideshoots to five leaves, and then to one or two buds in the winter. In subsequent years, treat as for a cordon.

Blackcurrants

Blackcurrants are grown as stooled bushes – that is, with a number of shoots growing from ground level. They fruit best on the previous year's growth, but will also crop on older wood.

Plant new bushes 2.5cm (1in) deeper than they had previously been grown, then cut back all shoots to 2.5cm (1in) from soil level.

For the first three years, if growth is strong, prune lightly in winter to remove just weak and low-lying growth. However, if growth is weak, prune harder, cutting at least half the shoots to ground level.

As bushes mature and start cropping, cut out one-third of the growth annually in winter, concentrating on old, unproductive wood, and weak and low-growing stems to promote strong growth from or near ground level. Other fruited branches can be cut back to vigorous sideshoots.

Blueberry buds – fruiting buds at the top, growth buds at the bottom. (Photo: Geoff Hodge)

Blueberries

The largest and best fruit is produced on the thick, vigorous shoots produced the previous spring or early summer. Any strong stems that appear in late summer may also produce fruit at the tips. Pruning should take place in late winter or early spring when the fruit buds are visible.

Young plants need little or no pruning in the first three years. Aim to produce an open-centred bush by removing weak growth and, of course, dead or diseased growth, also shoots that grow horizontally or are overly long. Prune to an upright shoot or healthy bud wherever possible.

On mature plants remove older stems lacking strength. Remove thin, twiggy growth, also crossing or horizontal shoots, or stems close to the ground. Cut back some branches to their base, and others to strong upright shoots. Stems that fruited the previous year should be pruned to a low, strong-growing upward-facing bud or shoot. By the end of pruning you should have cut out up to 15 per cent of the old growth.

Vine Fruit

All vine fruits are vigorous climbers that produce strong growth and need sturdy supports to grow up. When in fruit, their stems can become exceptionally heavy.

Pruning blackcurrant bushes

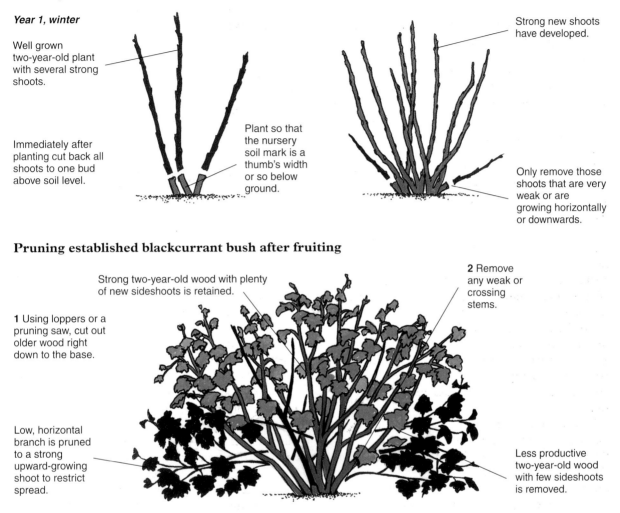

Year 1, winter

Well grown two-year-old plant with several strong shoots.

Immediately after planting cut back all shoots to one bud above soil level.

Plant so that the nursery soil mark is a thumb's width or so below ground.

Year 2, winter

Strong new shoots have developed.

Only remove those shoots that are very weak or are growing horizontally or downwards.

Pruning established blackcurrant bush after fruiting

Strong two-year-old wood with plenty of new sideshoots is retained.

2 Remove any weak or crossing stems.

1 Using loppers or a pruning saw, cut out older wood right down to the base.

Low, horizontal branch is pruned to a strong upward-growing shoot to restrict spread.

Less productive two-year-old wood with few sideshoots is removed.

To produce worthwhile crops they must be well trained, and the growth restricted by regular pruning; without this, the shoots become very tangled and the crop is reduced.

Grapes

Grape pruning can be seen as complicated and difficult – which in fact it generally is! But by carefully following an annual pruning regime you can easily achieve good crops.

Grapes must be pruned in mid-winter when they are dormant, otherwise they bleed sap – although it is possible to safely cut back soft annual growth and remove growing tips in summer. There are several training and pruning methods, but grapes are generally either trained on a cordon (indoor and dessert grapes) or a Guyot (outdoor, wine grapes) system. The vines will need to be supported on strong wires, usually spaced 30–40cm (12–16in) apart; for the Guyot system the lowest wire should be 40cm (16in) from ground level.

Cordons consist of permanent vertical arms and annual horizontal cropping shoots (rods), whereas the Guyot system consists of a short trunk with low, annually renewed horizontal arms and vertical cropping shoots.

Pruning grape vines (rod–and–spur system)

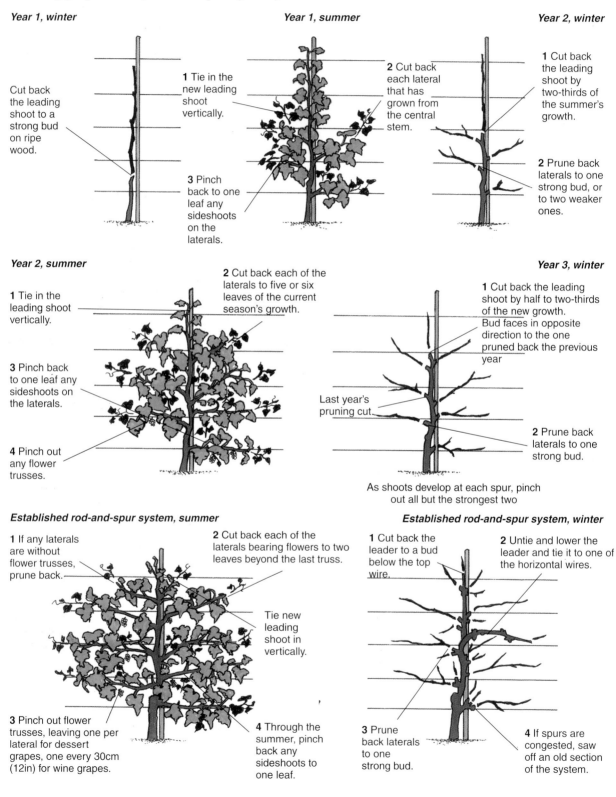

Year 1, winter

Cut back the leading shoot to a strong bud on ripe wood.

1 Tie in the new leading shoot vertically.

3 Pinch back to one leaf any sideshoots on the laterals.

Year 1, summer

2 Cut back each lateral that has grown from the central stem.

Year 2, winter

1 Cut back the leading shoot by two-thirds of the summer's growth.

2 Prune back laterals to one strong bud, or to two weaker ones.

Year 2, summer

1 Tie in the leading shoot vertically.

2 Cut back each of the laterals to five or six leaves of the current season's growth.

3 Pinch back to one leaf any sideshoots on the laterals.

4 Pinch out any flower trusses.

Year 3, winter

1 Cut back the leading shoot by half to two-thirds of the new growth. Bud faces in opposite direction to the one pruned back the previous year

Last year's pruning cut

2 Prune back laterals to one strong bud.

As shoots develop at each spur, pinch out all but the strongest two

Established rod-and-spur system, summer

1 If any laterals are without flower trusses, prune back.

2 Cut back each of the laterals bearing flowers to two leaves beyond the last truss.

Tie new leading shoot in vertically.

3 Pinch out flower trusses, leaving one per lateral for dessert grapes, one every 30cm (12in) for wine grapes.

4 Through the summer, pinch back any sideshoots to one leaf.

Established rod-and-spur system, winter

1 Cut back the leader to a bud below the top wire.

2 Untie and lower the leader and tie it to one of the horizontal wires.

3 Prune back laterals to one strong bud.

4 If spurs are congested, saw off an old section of the system.

Cordon or Rod-and-spur System

After planting, during winter, cut the leader to a strong bud on ripe, firm wood just above the first training wire. Cut back any sideshoots to two buds.

Throughout summer tie in the leader vertically, cut back laterals to five leaves and sideshoots on the laterals to two leaves. Remove any flowers.

In the second winter cut back the leader by as much as two-thirds of the summer's growth to leave only ripened, brown wood, pruning to a bud. Cut back laterals to one bud if it looks strong, or to two buds if it doesn't.

In the second summer, repeat the treatment of the first summer and during the third winter, repeat the treatment carried out in the second winter. Repeat the winter pruning in subsequent years until the leader reaches the top wire, thereafter pruning the leader to a bud at the top wire.

Each spring and summer allow laterals to form at each training wire, left and right of the main stem. If more than one lateral develops, pinch surplus shoots to one leaf. In winter cut back all laterals to two buds.

Remove any fruit in the first two years, and leave only three or four bunches in the third year. After this allow one bunch per 30cm (12in) length of rod, pinching shoots two leaves beyond the flower bunch, or five leaves for non-flowering shoots.

Guyot System

After planting, cut back the leader to about 15cm (6in) from the ground, leaving at least two or three good buds. Throughout the summer tie in the leader vertically, cut back the laterals to five leaves, and the sideshoots on the laterals to two leaves. Remove any flowers.

In the following winter, cut back the leading shoot to 40cm (16in), leaving three good buds. During the summer, train in three new shoots vertically. Tuck any sideshoots from these into the parallel wires to grow horizontally. Remove any other shoots growing from the base.

In the third winter, cut back the two outer shoots to 60cm (2ft) and carefully bend them to the bottom wire, tying one to the left and the other to the right. Then cut back the central stem to three or four buds to produce replacement rods (stems) for the following year.

In the third and subsequent summers, tie in shoots vertically from each horizontal arm, pinching out their tips at the top supporting wire. As sideshoots develop on the vertical shoots, pinch them out. Allow only three shoots to develop on the central arm and remove any others, cutting out any sideshoots that form on them to one leaf. Thin bunches of grapes to 30cm (12in) apart.

In subsequent winters, cut off the two horizontal arms and their vertical shoots. Then treat the three central shoots as in the third winter.

Thinning Dessert Grapes

Dessert grape bunches need thinning to ensure individual fruit size, sweetness and quality. The bunches are thinned using scissors, to increase the spacing between individual fruits; this allows each grape to develop to a good size, and allows sufficient air and light penetration between them to encourage even ripening and discourage problems with fungal diseases.

A primary thinning can be done while the grapes are very small, and a secondary thinning, if necessary, once the grapes have increased in size.

Kiwi Fruit

The kiwi fruit, or Chinese gooseberry (*Actinidia deliciosa*), isn't particularly frost hardy, and only crops reliably in warm, protected areas. Some hardier cultivars are available that fruit in cooler areas, but the fruit may be damaged by early frosts. They can be grown along pergolas, but training against a warm, sheltered south-facing wall will give the most reliable results outdoors. Plants can be grown in a greenhouse or conservatory, but their extensive growth means they need a large area – up to 10m (33ft) long. And although there are self-fertile cultivars, both female and pollinating male plants are needed. The males are more vigorous than the females, but can be cut back hard after flowering; one male plant will pollinate up to eight female plants. Fruit is produced on the previous year's growth and at the base of the current year's.

Pruning grape vines (Guyot system)

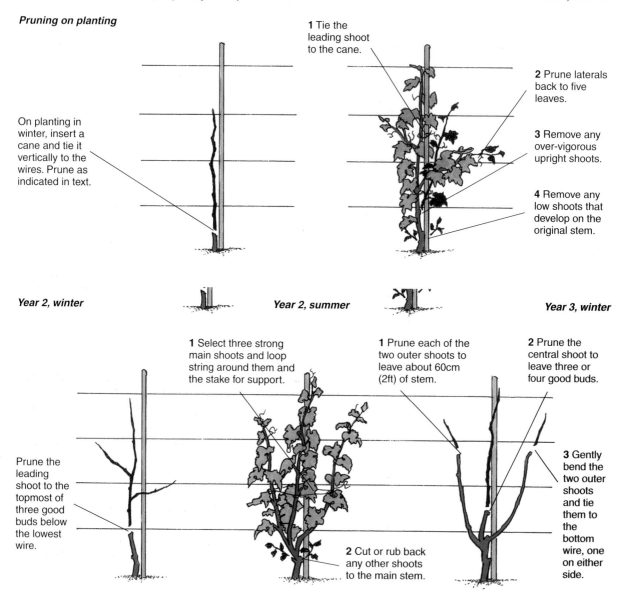

Pruning on planting

On planting in winter, insert a cane and tie it vertically to the wires. Prune as indicated in text.

Year 1, summer

1 Tie the leading shoot to the cane.

2 Prune laterals back to five leaves.

3 Remove any over-vigorous upright shoots.

4 Remove any low shoots that develop on the original stem.

Year 2, winter

Prune the leading shoot to the topmost of three good buds below the lowest wire.

Year 2, summer

1 Select three strong main shoots and loop string around them and the stake for support.

2 Cut or rub back any other shoots to the main stem.

Year 3, winter

1 Prune each of the two outer shoots to leave about 60cm (2ft) of stem.

2 Prune the central shoot to leave three or four good buds.

3 Gently bend the two outer shoots and tie them to the bottom wire, one on either side.

The best method of training is to produce an espalier with a central upright stem and tiers of horizontal stems trained on wires 45cm (18in) apart. Plant from autumn to early spring, and cut back the main stem to 30cm (12in) in late winter or early spring before growth starts. Tie in the developing leading shoot to a vertical cane tied to the wires. Tie in pairs of sideshoots to each horizontal wire on either side of the main stem; these will form the permanent fruiting branches or arms. When each arm is 90cm (3ft) long, pinch out its tip and retrain the leading shoot. Sideshoots will

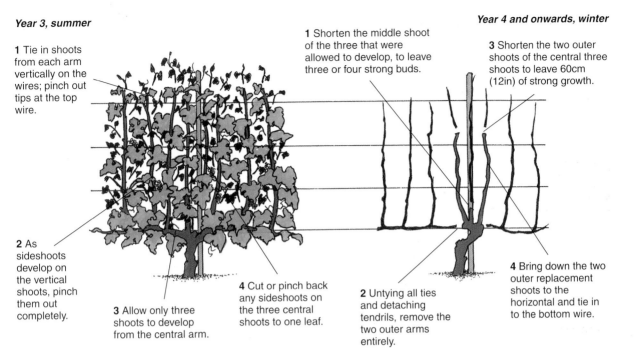

Year 3, summer

1 Tie in shoots from each arm vertically on the wires; pinch out tips at the top wire.

2 As sideshoots develop on the vertical shoots, pinch them out completely.

3 Allow only three shoots to develop from the central arm.

4 Cut or pinch back any sideshoots on the three central shoots to one leaf.

1 Shorten the middle shoot of the three that were allowed to develop, to leave three or four strong buds.

2 Untying all ties and detaching tendrils, remove the two outer arms entirely.

Year 4 and onwards, winter

3 Shorten the two outer shoots of the central three shoots to leave 60cm (12in) of strong growth.

4 Bring down the two outer replacement shoots to the horizontal and tie in to the bottom wire.

develop along the arms, and these should be pinched back after five or six leaves; any sideshoots they produce should be removed.

In the following year, fruit will form on the sideshoots and these should be pinched out five to seven leaves beyond the cluster of developing fruit; sideshoots that don't fruit should be cut back to four or five leaves. After harvesting, cut back the fruited shoots to two or three buds beyond the last fruit.

The fruiting sideshoots or spurs will usually fruit well for three or four years; after this time they should be cut back to buds near the main arms in winter.

Passion Fruit

The edible passion fruits (*Passiflora edulis* and other species) are not frost hardy, and only crop reliably in frost-free areas or, better still, within a conservatory or greenhouse.

There are numerous methods of training including along horizontal wires on a wall, up wire or plastic netting, around a tripod or along a pergola. Best results are obtained by training stems along horizontal supports in two directions. Fruit is produced on the current year's growth

Plants are trained and pruned in the same way as ornamental passion fruits; *see* page 73 for details.

Glossary

Adventitious bud Dormant bud on a stem, often invisible until stimulated into growth.

Alternate buds Stems or leaves alternating at different levels on opposite sides of the stem.

Annual A plant that germinates, grows, flowers and sets seeds all in one year.

Apex The tip of a stem.

Apical bud The bud at the tip of a stem.

Apical dominance The controlling influence of an apical bud over the growth of buds and shoots below.

Axil Where a leaf joins a stem.

Axillary bud A bud that occurs in an axil.

Bark-ringing The removal of a ring of bark from a trunk or shoot to reduce vigorous growth and help promote flowering and fruiting.

Basal shoots Shoots arising at or near ground level.

Bleeding The oozing of sap from a cut or wound.

Blind shoot A shoot that does not form a flower, or one where the growing point has been damaged or removed.

Blossom thinning The removal of some blossom on a fruiting plant to ensure a reasonable crop of good-sized fruit.

Bract A modified leaf at the base of a flower, which may be coloured and so resembles a flower petal.

Branch collar The thickened ring at the base of a branch.

Branch leader The leading shoot of a branch.

Branch-headed standard Tree with a clear trunk and a branched head or crown.

Brutting The technique often used on nut trees to break, but not sever, long sideshoots to restrict growth and encourage flowering.

Bud A condensed shoot containing an embryonic leaf, leaf cluster, flower or flowers.

Bud break The process of a leaf or shoot emerging from a bud.

Callus The protective tissue formed by plants covering a wound or wounded surface.

Central leader The main central stem of a plant.

Central-leader standard A tree or shrub with a clear stem that continues as the central leader through the crown of branches.

Controlled-release fertilizer A fertilizer that only releases its nutrients when conditions are right for plant growth.

Coppicing The process of regular pruning of trees or shrubs at or close to ground level to stimulate the growth of new shoots.

OPPOSITE: Pruning a redcurrant bush.
(Photo: Tim Sandall)

Cordon A plant trained to produce one main stem clothed in many short growths.

Crotch The angle between two branches or between a branch and a trunk.

Crown The branched part of a tree or standard shrub above the trunk or main stem.

Crown lifting The process of removing lower branches on a tree to produce a taller, clear trunk.

Crown reduction The process of reducing the size of a crown by cutting back the longest branches.

Crown thinning The process of removing crowded growth from within the crown of a tree.

Cultivar A cultivated variety that has originated in cultivation (usually from controlled breeding), rather than in the wild.

Deadheading The process of removing spent flowers or flower heads and the developing seed head.

Deciduous Plants that lose their leaves in autumn or winter.

Dieback The death of the tip of a shoot, often spreading further down the shoot.

Disbudding The process of removing surplus buds to help promote better flowers or fruit, or the removal of dormant buds.

Dormant bud A bud that is alive but inactive.

Dual leaders Competing leaders (main stems) of usually equal strength.

Epicormic shoot A shoot that develops from latent or adventitious buds under the bark of a tree or shrub (*see* **Water shoots**).

Espalier A trained plant with a vertical central stem and tiers of branches growing horizontally on either side.

Evergreen A plant that retains its foliage all year.

Extension growth New growth made to extend the length of a branch or stem.

Fan A pruned and trained tree with the main branches radiating in a fan shape from a short trunk.

Fastigiate A plant with branches growing vertically and almost parallel with the main stem.

Feathered maiden One-year-old tree that has produced lateral shoots (feathers).

Festooning A fruit-training technique where branches are tied down to a more horizontal position to help stimulate fruiting.

Foliar feed A liquid fertilizer that can be absorbed by the leaves as well as the roots.

Framework The permanent structure of branches of a tree or shrub.

Fruit thinning The removal of some developing fruit to improve the quality of those remaining.

Graft union The point at which a cultivar (the scion) is grafted on to a rootstock.

Grafting The process of joining the top growth of one plant (the scion) on to the roots of another (the rootstock).

Growing point The top bud of a shoot.

Growth bud A bud that develops into leaves or a shoot.

Half-hardy perennial A long-lived herbaceous plant that is unable to tolerate frost, but usually able to tolerate lower temperatures than a frost-tender plant.

Herbaceous perennial A long-lived plant that produces non-woody growth.

Internode The length of stem between two nodes.

Latent bud A dormant bud that may later be stimulated into growth.

Lateral Side growth that appears from any shoot or root.

Lateral bud Bud that will form a sideshoot.

Leader The main, usually central, upright, shoot.

Leading shoot The main central shoot.

Leg Short, clear length of stem before branching occurs.

Lorette system Method of summer-pruning apples and pears to restrict vegetative growth and promote fruiting growth.

Maiden A tree in its first year.

Maiden whip One-year-old tree that hasn't developed lateral branches (*see* **Feathered maiden** and **Whip**).

Maypoling Method by which branches heavily laden with fruit are prevented from breaking.

Mulch A layer of material added to the soil surface to suppress weeds, conserve soil moisture and maintain an even soil temperature.

Multi-stemmed Tree or shrub with several main stems, either arising directly from the soil or from a short main stem (leg).

Nicking The process of removing a semi-circle or small triangle of bark below a dormant bud to prevent its development (*see* **Notching**).

Node The point on a stem where leaves, shoots or flowers arise.

Notching The process of removing a semi-circle or small triangle of bark above a dormant bud to stimulate its development (*see* **Nicking**).

Opposite buds Buds at the same level on opposite sides of a stem.

Paring Trimming with a pruning knife.

Pinch pruning Method of pruning where soft shoot tips are removed, usually by thumb and forefinger.

Pinching back/Pinching out The process of pinching out soft growth tips to shape the plant's growth.

Pleaching A technique where branches from a row of trees are woven together and trained to form a narrow screen or canopy.

Pollard A tree that is cut back at regular intervals to the head of the main trunk.

Pollarding The process of regularly pruning back the main branches of a tree or shrub to the head of the main stem/trunk or, sometimes, to a short branch framework.

Prostrate Plant with stems growing along the ground.

Pyramid A training method for fruit trees in which each tier of branches is made up of shorter branches than the tier below.

Regulated pruning The occasional removal of branches or pieces of branches to prevent congestion and stimulate younger growth.

Remedial pruning The removal of dead, damaged, diseased or dying growth.

Renewal pruning The regular removal of older growth.

Renovation pruning The hard cutting back of an old plant, often to ground level, to stimulate new growth.

Replacement shoot A strong, young shoot that is trained or retained to replace older growth removed by pruning.

Reversion The production of shoots with all-green leaves on variegated plants.

Rib Main branch of a fan-trained tree

Rod A main stem of a grape vine.

Root pruning The process of removing some of the roots to restrict growth and promote flowering and fruiting.

Rootstock The plant used to provide the roots for a grafted plant.

Rubbing out The removal of unwanted buds or young shoots by hand.

Scion The plant, usually a cultivar, that is grafted on to the rootstock of another plant.

Secondary growth Growth that appears after pruning.

Semi-evergreen A plant that may retain its leaves in winter depending on the severity of the weather.

Sideshoot A shoot growing out from a stem.

Snag An overlong stub left behind after incorrect pruning.

Spur A small shoot or short branch bearing flowers or fruit.

Spur bearing A plant that produces its flowers and fruit on short shoots along the stem (*see* **Tip bearing**).

Spur pruning Shortening shoots to produce spurs to stimulate flower bud or fruit bud production.

Spur system Clusters of spurs produced by spur pruning.

Standard A tree or shrub with a clear stem below a head of branches.

Stool Several shoots appearing from the base of a plant, often as a result of pruning.

Stooling The regular pruning back of plants to ground level.

Stopping *See* **Pinching back**.

Sublateral Sideshoot on a lateral shoot.

Subshrub A shrub-like plant that is woody at the base but with soft, often herbaceous, growth above.

Sucker A shoot that appears at, or just below, ground level from a plant's root system or underground stem. On grafted plants it is any shoot that appears below the graft union and is therefore from the rootstock.

Tip bearing A plant that produces its flowers and fruit at or near the shoot tips (*see* **Spur bearing**).

Tip pruning The process of pinching out or cutting back the growing tip of a shoot to remove damaged growth and/or encourage sideshoots.

Trunk Thick, woody main stem of a tree.

Vegetative growth Growth that is non-flowering and usually leafy.

Water shoots Fast-growing, thin epicormic shoots. They usually form around pruning cuts or damaged areas.

Whip A young tree, consisting of a single stem that hasn't developed lateral branches (*see* **Maiden whip**).

Whorl The arrangement of three or more leaves or shoots arising from the same point.

Index